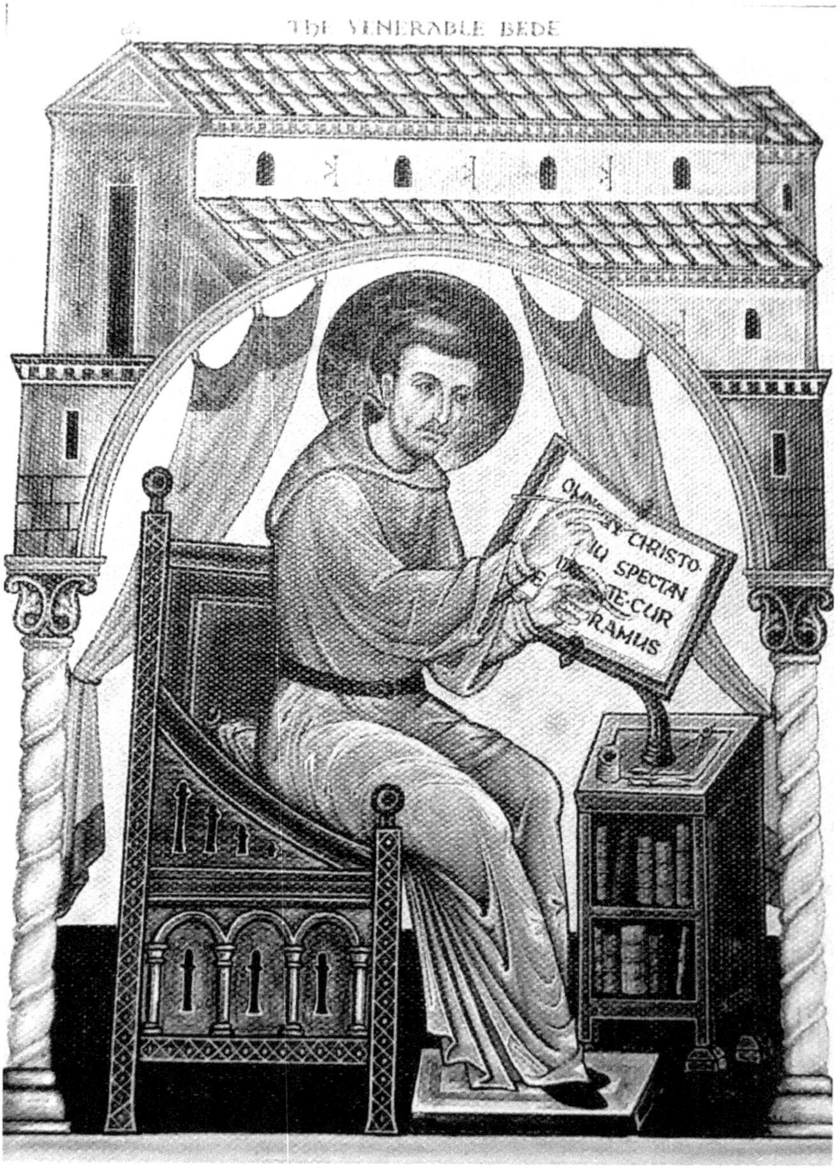

The Venerable Bede

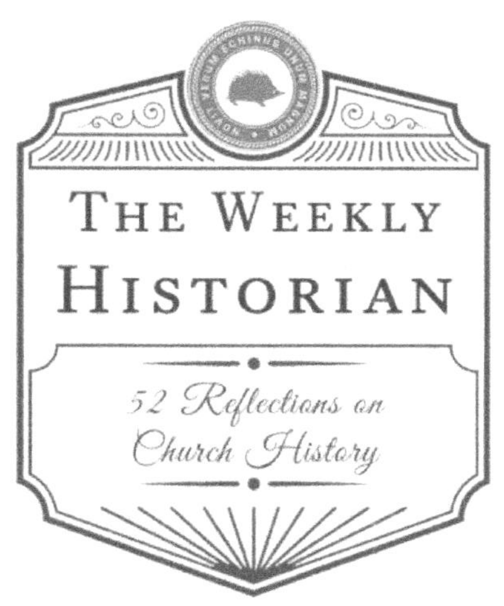

THE WEEKLY HISTORIAN

52 Reflections on Church History

MICHAEL A.G. HAYKIN

H&E
Publishing

To Matthew Hall and Hershael York once again:

For the joy of serving as a church historian at
The Southern Baptist Theological Seminary
under their leadership

Contents

Table of images

Introduction

A pithy remark by Caleb Evans, the eighteenth-century Baptist leader, which I read in the course of preparation for my doctoral comprehensive examinations in 1977–1978 has stayed with me over the years: "Every Christian ought to be a good historian." At the time I had no idea who Evans was, nor the significance of his life and ministry for the English Baptist cause in his day. He made this remark in the course of a sermon that he preached on November 5, 1778, which was entitled *The Remembrance of Former Days*. November 5 was the day that the Roman Catholic Guy Fawkes' plot to blow up the Houses of Parliament in 1605 was discovered and foiled. It was also the day when William of Orange landed in Torbay in 1688 and went on to execute a successful coup d'état against his father-in-law, the Catholic James II, and so ensured that the British throne would remain within the realm of Protestantism. So, for these two reasons, ardent Protestants like Evans in the eighteenth century celebrated the remembrance of these momentous events with an annual sermon and worship. Evans' 1778 sermon was a call to his "ordinary" Christian hearers to read history and remember it, for in truth they were surrounded by its impact day after day. In Evans' words: "Every Christian ought to be a good historian, and if his knowledge of history be improved by him as it ought, the better historian he is, the better Christian will he be."

Well, this weekly reader is designed to help you become "a good historian" in the way that Evans desired. These 52 weekly reflections, each of which takes but a few minutes to read, are a reminder of how important history—in this case, actually, church history—is for the believer. The first reading for the first week of the year is actually a mini-defence of why we should read church history regularly. The remaining 51 reflections then go through the Patristic and Medieval eras (Weeks 2–16), the sixteenth-century Reformation (Weeks 17–32), Puritanism and early Evangelicalism to the close of the eighteenth century (Weeks 33–49), with the remaining three reflections focused on people and events of the late nineteenth and early twentieth centuries (Weeks 50–52). These weekly reflections very much mirror eras in which I am especially interested and about which I have written widely: late Antiquity and evangelical Protestantism from the Reformation to the long eighteenth century.

If this book were intended to be an overview of church history, it would be quite inadequate. But it is not meant to be a survey of church history. Rather, consider it a taster of the riches of the past history of Christianity, which hopefully will lead you to further reading and discoveries. There are also some common themes that appear, which again reflect my doctrinal interests: biblicism, the Trinity and pneumatology, the need for revival. Again, these hardly exhaust the riches of Christian thought. They are meant to spur you on to reflect upon the way Christians have thought upon other vital matters, such as Christology, ethics, and political theology. Finally, given the nature of this weekly reader, I have not included in its pages the dates of the various figures I refer to and cite (these can be easily found online). Nor have I retained that key element of my apparatus as an academic historian, the footnote or endnote. I do quote various historical figures and contemporary historians, but because of the nature of this work (and the way that the reflections originally appeared), I have chosen not to include either footnotes or endnotes.

Most of these reflections appeared first in a monthly column that I have been privileged to write for the English Christian newspaper, *Evangelicals Now* (https://www.e-n.org.uk/), and are gratefully reprinted here by permission. A few of the others had their origin on a blog that I once maintained, *Historia ecclesiastica* (named after the famous work by the Anglo-Saxon historian Bede, whose picture graces the frontispiece of the book). And finally, one or two originated in *Tabletalk*, the Bible study magazine of Ligonier Ministries, which are also reprinted by kind permission.

The images in the book are in the public domain, having been taken from Wikimedia Commons or the New York Public Library bank of digitized images. A few are from the author's private collection. One image, that of Katherine Willoughby, the Duchess of Suffolk, is used by permission of Alamy.

1
"Every Christian ought to be a good historian"

Though it was written two hundred years ago, Jane Austen's fiction is still popular since so much of it still rings true to human experience. In her novel *Northanger Abbey* (1817), for instance, the heroine Catherine Morland makes a statement that is amazingly prescient about the modern boredom with history. In Catherine's words, history "tells me nothing that does not either vex or weary me. The quarrels of popes and kings, with wars or pestilences, in every page; the men all so good for nothing, and hardly any women at all—it is very tiresome." Many in the modern world, sadly even Christians, see the past as little more than this: a tiresome account of a few big names with little wisdom to impart for life today. At best, it may offer a couple of hours of entertainment and diversion via a movie or a novel.

History, important to God

How different is the Bible's perspective on the past. Here, history is obviously important to God, since it is the realm where God ultimately brings about the salvation of his people by entering into the very fabric of time and taking on our humanity, sin excepted, in the person of Jesus Christ. This divine activity in the realm of history should not be restricted to the Bible. Though it is impossible to trace out his footsteps across the sands of time in detail, it is blasphemous to deny that God is at work. His work may often be hidden, but it is biblical to confess that he is providentially guiding history for the glory of his Name and the good of his people. As such, to quote the seventeenth-century Puritan Richard Baxter, "The writing of Church-history is the duty of all ages, because God's works are to be known, as well as his Word." Reading Church history should lead therefore to the praise of God and his adoration.

The individual and history

Men and women are historical beings, immersed in the flow of time. Without the past our lives have little or no meaning. When a community forgets its past, it is like a person suffering from dementia: they really cannot function in the world. So we must study history, and as Christians, this means Church history.

This reading of the history of God's people can also provide us with models for imitation. For instance, in Hebrews 11–12:2, the writer uses the history of God's faithful people in the old covenant to encourage his readers to run the "foot-race" of faith. He wants them to draw encouragement from the lives of past believers to press on in faith and obedience towards the final goal.

And we soon discover that this story of the past is not simply that of an elite few, but encompasses every believer's life and that we can learn as much from the so-called minor figures of Church History as from the "big names." As the American apologist Francis Schaeffer reminds us: with God there are no little people!

History—a path to humility & freedom
Studying church history also builds a deep sense of indebtedness to others who have gone before us, and thus helps to cultivate the great virtue of humility. The study of our past informs us about our predecessors in the faith, those who have helped shape our Christian communities and thus make us what we are. Such study builds humility and modesty into our lives, and so can exercise a sanctifying influence upon us. Jesus put it this way in John 4: "Others have laboured, and you have entered into their labour" (ESV).

The study of Church history also liberates us from the tyranny of present-day ideas, what C.S. Lewis calls "the idols of our marketplace." Consider Francis of Assisi's attitude towards poverty. For him the word "poverty" (*paupertas*) was a bride to be embraced since he believed that it gave him true freedom. For modern Westerners, Christian and pagan alike, poverty is generally viewed as an unmitigated economic disaster that places severe limitations on one's freedom. This example reveals the way that Church History can call into question what we take for granted as an absolute and reveal it to be merely relative and culture-bound.

Little wonder then that the eighteenth-century, evangelical Baptist Caleb Evans once said that "every Christian ought to be a good historian."

2
On papyrus

The Bible is bound up with history in many ways. One of them is the basic way that the Bible has come down to us. The most prominent medium by which the Scriptures were recorded for us was on papyrus, which is largely unique to the Nile Delta in Egypt and began to be used for writing books as far back as the third millennium BC.

Making the papyrus scroll
Papyrus is a reed that grows between 7 and 16 feet in height and has a long three-sided stalk without joints, which is roughly the thickness of the human wrist. It is amazing to think that someone in the third millennium looked at this plant and thought, "I could use that for writing." Due to its vital use in recording the Scriptures, one can see the providential hand of God at work in its discovery as a medium for writing.

To make it into a writing material, the hard, outer shell was cut away. This revealed the softer pithy centre, which the Greek called *biblos*, the word from which our term "Bible" ultimately derives. This centre was then cut into thin strips. These were placed side by side on a hard, smooth surface, while other strips were placed at right angles in a layer over them. These two layers were then fused by means of a press that broke down the cellular structure of the papyrus fibres and released the juice of the pithy centre that acted as a glue. This formed a sheet that was then dried, trimmed, and the surface smoothed out with pumice. The size of a single sheet ranged from 4 inches to 11 inches in width and from 8 inches to a foot in length. For a biblical reference to a single sheet, see 2 John 12.

The next step in the manufacturing process was to paste individual sheets together to form a longer strip, which was then rolled up as a scroll with wooden dowels at either end. One side had the fibres running horizontally—this would be called the recto. The other side, which had the fibres running vertically, was called the verso. A flour paste was used to join the separate sheets.

A standard roll had about twenty sheets and ran to about eleven and a half feet. The strip of glued sheets was rolled up with the recto, the intended side for writing, facing inwards for protection. Writing on both sides of the papyrus was quite unusual. It is thus interesting that the scroll mentioned in Revelation 5:1 was "written on the inside [the recto] and on the back [the verso]."

It is reckoned that the two longest books of the New Testament—Luke and Acts—would have filled scrolls of about 30 to 32 feet in length. Not surprisingly, one of the librarians at the famed Library of Alexandria, Callimachus, used to say, "A big book [scroll] is a big nuisance"

Once a papyrus scroll was produced, it was often often wrapped in cloth or leather and stored in some kind of container, usually a jar.

Alexandria and books

Since most papyrus grew in the Nile Delta, Egypt eventually came to supply papyrus for the most of the Mediterranean world and it became a major book production centre. In fact, the library of Alexandria was deemed one of the wonders of the Ancient World and made Alexandria a centre for scholarship.

The great third-century Bible exegete Origen, who played a critical role in the defence of the Old Testament as Scripture in the face of the rejection of it by the various heretical groups known as the Gnostics, did much of his early studies in this remarkable city.

The autographs

All of the original copies of the books of the New Testament, which scholars call "autographs," were written on papyrus. Currently, there are 97 papyri of various portions of the New Testament extant. The oldest is called p^{52}—which dates from AD 125—and contains a portion of the Gospel of John, namely, John 18:31–33, 37–38. Virtually no other book from the Ancient World is so well attested as our New Testament.

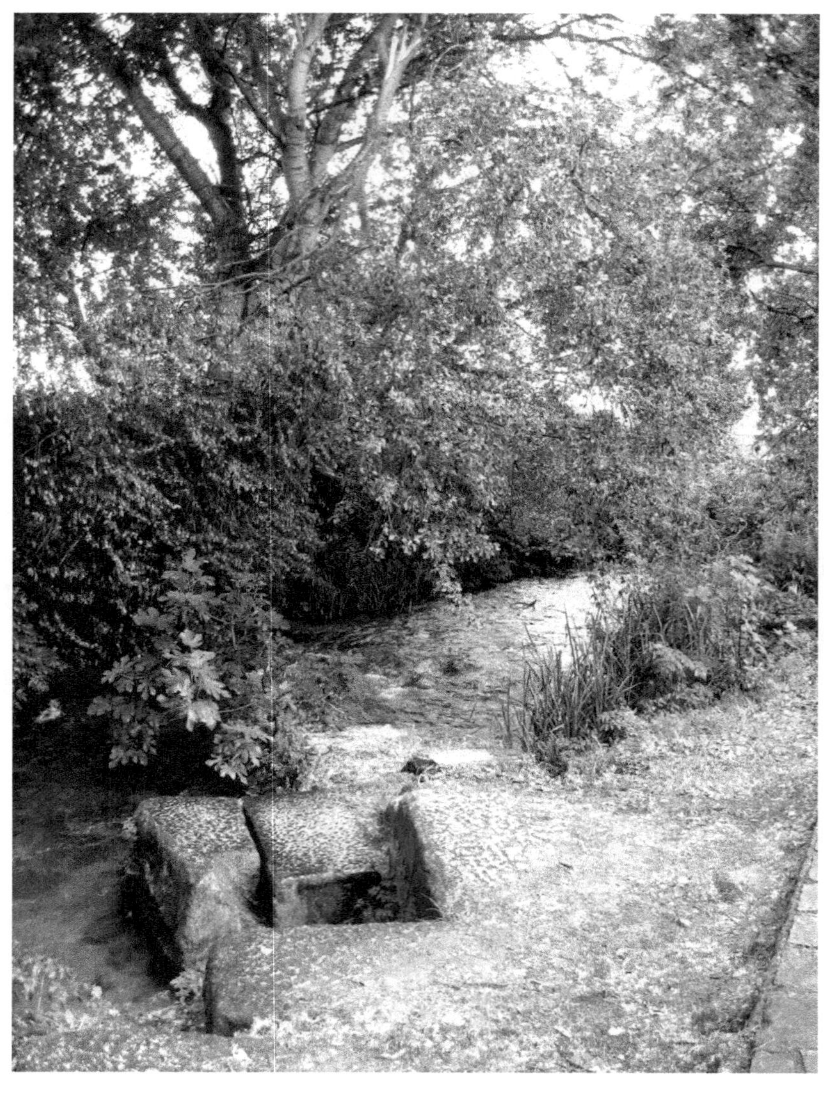

The supposed site of Lydia's baptism

3

A "frantic passion for purple":
ancient fashion, snails,
and the advance of the Gospel

In 1856, English Chemistry student William Henry Perkin was looking for a cure for malaria—he stumbled upon a way to make a synthetic purple dye from coal tar instead. In so doing, he literally changed history, for his discovery led to advances in medicine, photography, perfumery, food production, and revolutionized the fashion industry.

Making ancient Tyrian purple
Purple has long been valued as a colour, because, for many years, obtaining it entailed a monumental difficulty. According to the Roman scientist Pliny the Elder, who died in the eruption of Vesuvius in AD 79, the best purple dye in the Ancient Near East was manufactured at the Phoenician city of Tyre (for the association of Tyre with purple dye, see 2 Chronicles 2:7). The raw material out of which this dye was manufactured was obtained from the glandular secretion—or tears, as the Christian commentator Isidore of Seville poetically put it—of a carnivorous sea snail, which contemporary science knows as the *Murex bandaris*. Somewhere around 12,000 of these snails had to be harvested from the sea to produce merely 0.05 of an ounce of dye. A foul stench emanated from the Phoenician factories manufacturing the dye; understandably they were situated on the outskirts of the city. Tyrian purple, as it was known, was literally worth more than its weight in gold and purple-dyed fabrics commanded exorbitant prices. As Pliny noted of ancient fashion, "it adds radiance to every garment," and this led to what he called a "frantic passion for purple" among the upper and middle classes of his world. The Old Testament world of the Ancient Near East had been similarly shaped by this passion for purple, where it was associated with royalty and prestige and power (see, for example, Proverbs 31:22; Song of Solomon 3:9–10, 7:5; Daniel 5:7; Esther 8:15).

The Christian seller of purple

So, what does this ancient purple dye have to do with the Gospel? Well, in Luke's Book of Acts we read that when the apostle Paul came to the city of Philippi in AD 49, he met a woman named Lydia, who was originally from the city of Thyatira in the Roman province of Asia (modern-day Turkey). Ethnically she was Greek, but she had come to believe that the Jewish Old Testament contained the truth about God and the world, and thus she regularly met with a number of sincere Jewish women to pray and worship (Acts 16:14–15).

We are also told by Luke that she was "a dealer in purple" (verse 14), which meant that she either sold the dye, or, more likely, sold purple-dyed clothing. Either way, she would have been a woman of wealth and substance. Her regeneration by the Holy Spirit—"the Lord opened her heart" (verse 14)—led to her baptism and to her encouraging Paul to use her home as a base of mission in the city of Philippi.

If one reads through the Book of Acts it is apparent that when Paul went with the Gospel to a new city, a key part of his mission strategy was to find a place where the churches that were founded through the preaching of the Gospel could meet for distinctively Christian worship and fellowship. So it was that in Philippi, the Lord used the wealth that Lydia had obtained by the selling of purple clothing to rich and elite women—women who had a "frantic passion for purple"—to serve Paul's preaching and teaching about the Lord Christ.

The God who so made the *Murex bandaris* that its glands contained the base for purple appears to have had a greater purpose in mind than the making of a snail, glorious though that was!

4

Confessing the deity of the Holy Spirit

2025 will be the 1700th anniversary of the Council of Nicaea that was designed to bring an end to what historians call the Arian controversy, namely, the controversy engendered by the denial of the deity of both the Lord Jesus and the Holy Spirit by an Alexandrian elder named Arius in the late 310s. Instead, it initiated a further sixty years of intense theological reflection and controversy and led eventually to the promulgation of the Creed of Constantinople (381) in which the full divinity of Christ and his Spirit are confessed, and implicitly the formula—one God in three persons—taken as essential grammar for our speaking about God.

Confessing the deity of the Holy Spirit
In the final stage of this controversy (358–380) the focus was on the deity of the Holy Spirit. And it was the writings of the fourth-century Cappadocian Fathers—Basil of Caesarea, his brother Gregory of Nyssa, their close friend Gregory of Nazianzus, and Nazianzen's cousin Amphilochius of Iconium—that played a critical role in elucidating for the Church the biblical data regarding the person and deity of the Holy Spirit. One of the arguments that they brought forth for the deity of the Holy Spirit was based on the fact that he is designated in the New Testament as holy.

This connection between the Spirit's innate holiness and his deity is clearly brought out in a letter that Basil of Caesarea wrote in 373:

> We glorify the Holy Spirit together with the Father and the Son, from the conviction that he is not separated from the divine nature: what is foreign by nature does not share in the same honors. … [For] the creature is sanctified; the Spirit sanctifies. Whether you name angels, archangels, or all the heavenly powers, they receive their sanctification through the Spirit, but the Spirit has his holiness by nature, not as received by grace, but essentially his. From this, he has received the distinctive name of Holy. What then is by nature holy, as the Father is by nature holy and the Son by nature holy, we do not allow to be separated and severed from the divine and blessed

Trinity (*Letter* 159.2).

At the heart of this argument for the divine transcendence of the Spirit is the fact that he sanctifies others, for only that which is holy by nature—and thus divine—can sanctify another.

Holiness: a divine attribute

Basil rightly understood that innate holiness is a divine quality. In a study of the concept of holiness in the ancient world, Hannah K. Harrington maintains that for pre-Christian and first-century Judaism, "holiness describes God more closely than any other designation. His very essence is holiness. One could say that holiness is God's 'innermost reality' to which all of his His attributes are related." To describe God as holy was, for these Jews, to speak of his transcendent perfection and, in Harrington's words, to speak of his "exalted, powerful otherness that brings people to both admire and fear him."

When the New Testament, therefore, describes the Spirit of God as the "Holy Spirit" (1 Thessalonians 4:8), "the Spirit, the Holy One" (Ephesians 4:30), or as Romans 1:4 puts it, "the Spirit of holiness," a profound statement is being made about the nature of the Spirit. Since innate holiness belongs only to God, to call the Spirit "holy" implies that he is holy by nature and must be divine. This is quite a contrast to inter-testamental Judaism, which rarely uses the epithet of holy for the Spirit. And when the term "Holy Spirit" is found in inter-testamental Judaism it refers more often than not to a "God-given disposition to holiness" and principle of obedience, and not the Spirit of God. Harrington suggests, rightly in the mind of this author, that the reason why "the Rabbis do not refer overly much to the Holy Spirit" is due to the Spirit's "strong personification as a separate divine being in early Christianity."

While there is no extended discussion in the New Testament of the Spirit's nature, the arguments of the Cappadocian Fathers for the full divinity of the Holy Spirit's person rightly interpreted and intuited what is presupposed throughout the whole of the New Testament: the Spirit is fully God and therefore worthy of divine honors.

5

Converted by the Word of God:
the example of Hilary of Poitiers

Sociologist Rodney Stark has estimated that the number of professing Christians grew in the first three centuries from roughly a few thousand around 40AD, comprising .0017% of the population—based on an estimated population of 60 million in the entire Roman Empire—to over 6,000,000 by 300AD, roughly 10.5% of the total population, assuming the size of the population remained fairly stable.

Why did such growth take place? While a number of reasons need to be cited to answer this question, central to this growth—in a day when there was no public mass evangelism apart from what the martyrs shared before death—were the Scriptures. English Bible scholar Michael Green, commenting on this fact, has noted:

> From the Acts of the Apostles down to … Origen we find the same story repeated time and again. Discussion with Christians, arguments with them, annoyance at them, could lead enquirers to read these "barbaric writings" [i.e. the Scriptures] for themselves. And once they began to read, the Scriptures exercised their own fascination and power. Many an interested enquirer like Justin and Tatian, Athenagoras and Theophilus, came to Christian belief through finding, as he read, that "the Word of God is living and active and sharper than any two-edged sword" and that "the sacred Scriptures are able to instruct you for salvation through faith in Jesus Christ."

Hilary, a seeker after truth
One early Christian who knew the power and impact of the Word of God in his life was Hilary, born around 316 into a non-Christian home in Poitiers, Aquitaine, and who died in either 367 or 368. He probably became a Christian in his early twenties and went on to serve as a Christian bishop and author. In a very important book that he wrote entitled *On the Trinity* (356–60), he recalled at the beginning of the book how he had been led to Christ.

He records that he had been seeking for truth amidst the various religious options in the Roman world, when, in his words, he "chanced upon those books which according to Jewish tradition were written by Moses and the Prophets," namely, the Old Testament. As he read them, he became convinced that there is one true God, the Maker and origin of all things, who fills the entire universe, but who cannot be identified with his creation. This knowledge, he tells us, filled his soul with joy. It was a knowledge he readily confessed God had taught him.

Longing for eternal joy
But he longed for more. He longed, in his words, for a "hope of everlasting happiness." For, he reasoned, what good would there be in "thinking correctly about God if death were to destroy all sensation" and all thought. In fact, he began to think that it would not be right for God to have given him knowledge about his aseity, omnipotence and omnipresence if "his life might one day end and his death last for all eternity."

Hilary does not tell us how it was that he began to read the New Testament, what he calls this "evangelical and apostolic doctrine." But he did, and he began to read in the Gospel of John, the first chapter, verses 1 to 14. As he read of the fact that God made the universe by One who is here called the Word and who came into this world and took on human flesh, Hilary says "my fearful and anxious soul found greater hope than it had anticipated." Hilary came to see that the Word or the Son, or as he is often called in the New Testament, the Lord Jesus Christ, came into this world was so that he might die for sinners like himself and so that

> we may be raised from death to immortality with him. ... He allows himself to be nailed to the cross in order that by the curse of the cross all the curses of our earthly condemnation might be nailed to it and obliterated. ... Hence, we are born again by God in Christ through his death.

At last, he said, "my soul was at rest," conscious now of his security in Christ and "full of joy" as he contemplated the future. He began to share with others what he had come to believe for himself that they too might be saved. And he could now say that he had no greater reward than to serve

God by proclaiming him to a pagan world that did not know him.

AN EXTRACT

FROM THE

HOMILIES

OF

MACARIUS.

From John Wesley's *A Christian Library*

6

Introducing Macarius

In one of John Wesley's sermons, "The Scripture-Way of Salvation," the eighteenth-century Methodist leader sought to sum up his vision of the way of salvation as well as correct certain misunderstandings of this view of the Christian life. At one point, Wesley was concerned to stress that in the overwhelming experience of conversion it was natural for those who go through it to think that they are done with sin: "How easily do they draw that inference, 'I *feel* no sin; therefore I *have* none.'" But soon, Wesley stressed, "Temptations return and sin revives, showing that it was but stunned before, not dead. They now feel two principles in themselves, plainly contrary to each other: 'the flesh lusting against the spirit.'" Wesley then cited an obscure fourth-century monastic author whom he called Macarius to support his point.

John Wesley and Macarius
Wesley had been introduced to a German translation of Macarius' sermons in the colony of Georgia at the close of July, 1736, by some Moravian friends. The major themes of these sermons nicely dovetailed with Wesley's own interests, for in them Macarius especially set forth the saving work of the Holy Spirit and explored the experience of the believer, who, though indwelt by the Spirit, nevertheless battles indwelling sin.

In his diary, Wesley said that upon reading Macarius' sermons, he was moved with deep joy. In fact, Wesley so appreciated these homilies that he would later edit and reprint some of them in the first volume of his *A Christian Library*, a collection of Christian literature designed for lay preachers.

My own experience of reading Macarius mirrors that of Wesley: these are some of the richest texts of Christian spirituality in the history of the church and need to be better known. So, this week we outline what we know about Macarius and over the following two weeks we shall explore what he teaches about conversion and the life of the Christian.

Who was Macarius?

While there is much that is unclear about Macarius, the author of these works, he appears to have been especially active between the 380s and the 420s. He had strong ties to Syrian Christianity, although his mother tongue was most likely Greek. He would thus have been very comfortable with the theological worlds of both Syriac and Greek Christianity. His ministry seems to have been situated on the frontier of the Roman Empire in upper Syria and in southern Asia Minor, where he was the spiritual mentor to a number of monastic communities.

Four collections of his sermons are extant. They have been historically linked to a movement called Messalianism, an ascetic movement that was condemned at various councils. According to those who condemned them, the Messalians argued that there was an indwelling demonic power in each human soul, and that only intense and ceaseless prayer could break the power that this demonic power held over the soul. Consequently, they were said to refuse to work so that they could devote their entire time to prayer. They were also said to affirm physical experiences of the Spirit, and made light of the sacraments of the church as well as the ministry of those in official positions of power. The Messalians seems to have laid too much stress on their experience of the Spirit for the liking of official leaders in the Church.

Links to Basil and Gregory

Although there are a number of clear points of contact between the Messalians and Macarius, especially with regard to Macarius' deep interest in the Spirit, the burden of current scholarly opinion is that Macarius cannot be regarded as a Messalian. Confirmation of this perspective is found in Macarius' strong connections to two orthodox theologians, namely Basil of Caesarea and his brother Gregory of Nyssa, both of whom deeply admired Macarius. It was this connection with these two theologians that undoubtedly helped preserve the Macarian sermons.

Like these two theologians, Macarius had a profound concern to defend the deity of the Spirit. Macarius' sermons are profoundly Trinitarian, with a particular focus on the deity of the Holy Spirit. For

Macarius, the Spirit is "uncreated" and fully divine for he is the One who brings us into union with God.

7

Macarius on being human

When Macarius thought about the human state, what first came to his mind was the awful devastation caused by the fall of Adam and the reality of the tyranny of sin that ensued for his progeny as a result of his disobedience. Prior to the fall, Adam was clothed with the glory of the Holy Spirit, and thus knew the Spirit's personal instruction as well as that of the Word of God—the "Word was everything to him." He lived in total purity, was pleasing to God in all areas of his life and he had sovereign control over his thoughts and actions.

When he disobeyed God's Word of his own free will, though, his disobedience became the doorway through which all kinds of evil were sowed in the world, as well as being the vehicle for the entrance of "tumult, confusion, and battle" into the inner being of men and women. After the fall, Adam and his descendants lost both God and their God-given beauty.

Men and women were now marred by corruption, spiritual ugliness, and "a great stench" that emanated from their souls. Fallen men and women were now, in one of Macarius' most trenchant descriptions, like "houses of prostitution and ill-fame in which all sorts of immoral debaucheries go on." Instead of their Maker being their Lord, Satan himself became their prince and ruler, and filled their hearts with spiritual darkness.

Satan's domain

Ever true to his nature as a wicked tyrant, Satan did not spare any area of human existence from his deadly touch and control. The "evil prince corrupted" the human frame "completely, not sparing any of its members from its slavery, not its thoughts, neither the mind nor the body."

When men and women act under the impulse of these evils, they think that they are doing so on the basis of their "own determination." But from Macarius' vantage-point, every fallen human being is so under sin's dominion that he or she can "no longer see freely but sees evilly, hears evilly, and has swift feet to perpetrate evil acts."

Free will

Although this extremely realistic view of the Fall and its impact would appear to commit Macarius to a strongly determinist perspective with regard to the human condition, Macarius vehemently maintained that men and women are responsible for their actions.

But they cannot remove the deeply-rooted interiority of sin itself. Its dominion within the human heart is far too strong to be defeated by human energy alone. It is "impossible," Macarius stated on one occasion, "to separate the soul from sin unless God should calm and turn back this evil wind, inhabiting both the soul and body."

Again, as he put it elsewhere: "without the Lord Jesus and the working of divine power," that is, the Holy Spirit, "no one can ... be a Christian."

The sweetness of the Spirit

This situation can only be changed for the better, in Macarius' thinking, through a person persistently crying out to God for help to transform him or her from "bitterness to sweetness." So it is that Macarius can argue that "even the man ... completely immersed in sin and making himself a vessel of the devil ... has freedom to become a chosen vessel." Given Macarius' views about the devastation that has resulted from the Fall, some of which has been detailed above, this statement must be taken to mean that Macarius believes human beings have enough freedom to cry out to God for salvation.

Without the life-giving power of the Spirit, one is dead "as far as the kingdom goes, being unable to do any of the things of God," for "the Spirit is the life of the soul." And so great is the plague of sin in the human heart, healing is only found through the medicine of the Holy Spirit.

This gift of the Spirit in conversion, though, is only the beginning of what formed a major aspect of Macarius' theological reflections, namely, the remarkable nature of life in the Spirit, as we shall see next week.

8

Macarius on the sweetness of being a Christian

When Macarius thinks of the Christian life, the word that comes most readily to his mind is "joy." Sometimes the believer's life is flooded with the joy of the Spirit and he is like "a spouse who enjoys conjugal union with her bridegroom." On other occasions, he finds himself overwhelmed by grief as he prays in accordance with the "love of the Spirit towards mankind." Other times there is "a burning of the Spirit" which enflames the heart with regard to the things of God. Then, just as "deep, conjugal love" between man and a woman lead them to marry and leave father and mother and all other earthly loves, so "true fellowship with the Holy Spirit, the heavenly and loving Spirit" ultimately brings freedom from the loves of this age.

It bears noting that the gift of the Spirit is dependent on the cross-work of Christ. Likening the cross to the work of a gardener, Macarius argued that through the cross, Christ, "the heavenly and true gardener," removed from the barren soul "the thorns and thistles of evil spirits" as well as uprooting and burning with fire "the weeds of sin." With the removal of these, he can now plant in the soul "the most beautiful paradise of the Spirit." The gift of the Spirit is a fruit of the death of Christ.

Macarius thinks about the cross in primarily two ways. On the one hand, the cross is a place of healing and Christ is "the true physician" who has come to heal "everyone afflicted by the incurable wound of sin." Then, the cross is conceived of as a place of ransom, where Christ's life is given in payment for those of sinners. Thus, Macarius argued that Christ's blood was poured out on the cross so that there would be "life and deliverance for humanity." Again, he could state that Christ came to earth to "suffer on behalf of all and to buy them back with his blood."

Rivers of dragons and mouths of lions and dark forces
The gift of the indwelling Spirit, though, does not mean that the one whom he indwells is now exempt from spiritual warfare, for, "where the Holy Spirit is, there follows … persecution and struggle." As Marcus Plested

has noted, Macarius argued for "a profoundly militant Christianity." There is persecution of the Church by the powers of this age. The faithful believer is "nailed to the cross of Christ" and knows what it is to experience "the stigmata and wounds of the Lord." And there is struggle within the heart of the Christian, such that even the most mature Christian can fall back into a life of sin. In part, Macarius argued, this is because of the malice of Satan, who is "without mercy and hates humans," and thus never hesitates to attack Christians. In part, though, it is because Christians, even "those who are intoxicated with God" and "bound by the Holy Spirit," are not under constraint to do that which pleases God, for they still have their free will. Thus, Macarius read Ephesians 4:30 to mean that it was up to Christians' "will and freedom of choice to honour the Holy Spirit and not to grieve him" through sin.

Macarius personally knew men who seemed to be making great progress in the Christian life and then, through yielding to sin, lost everything. One man, who was a Roman aristocrat, seeking to follow Christ, sold his possessions and freed all of his slaves. He soon gained a reputation for being a holy man. Pride entered in and eventually he "fell completely into debaucheries and a thousand evils." Yet another suffered as a confessor under the rulers of imperial Perisa. He was horribly tortured. While in prison, a Christian woman sought to minister to him, but tempted by sexual lust, they "fell into fornication." The Christian experience of life in the Spirit in this world was thus one of great struggle against evil powers, whom, in a memorable turn of phrase, Macarius likened to "rivers of dragons and mouths of lions and dark forces."

Ultimately, though, it is not the human will that is the determinant factor in perseverance. It is "the power of the divine Spirit" that is the critical necessity for a person to attain to eternal life. True to the pneumatological focus in much of his thought, Macarius thus concluded: "if [a person] thinks he can effect a perfect work by himself without the help of the Spirit, he is totally in error. Such an attitude is unbecoming one who strives for heavenly places, for the kingdom."

A concluding word
Macarius' vision of the Christian life then is one of victorious liberation

from the tyranny of sin by the power of the Spirit of Christ. It begins with a heart dominated by evil, due to Adam's disobedience. Conversion brings liberty from this dreadful state of affairs, but plunges the believer into a warfare with indwelling sin and external spiritual enemies. Although the human will is now truly free to follow Christ or go back into a life of sin, ultimately it is the grace of the Spirit that spells victory in this war.

In many ways, Macarius' homilies are not marked by the deep theological sophistication of his contemporary Gregory of Nyssa, whom he influenced and who, like Macarius, was deeply interested in the twin themes of theological anthropology and pneumatology. Nevertheless, Macarius' deeply realistic approach to the human condition, his emphasis on the vital necessity of the Holy Spirit to effect eternal transformation, and his desire to take seriously human responsibility reveal him to be a thinker worthy of attention in our day that is also marked by a fascination with spirituality and a passionate interest in what it means to be truly human.

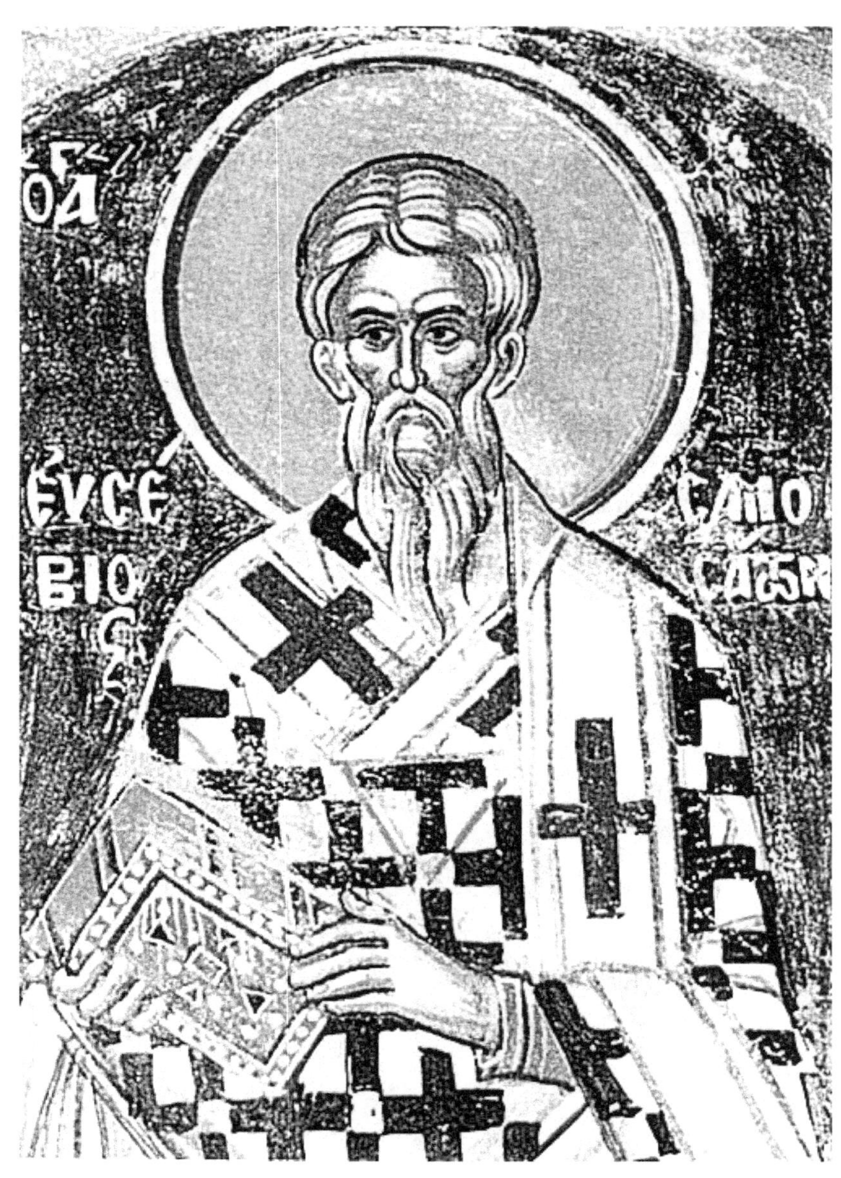

Eusebius of Samosata

9

"Very sweet honey":
Basil of Caesarea's friendship with Eusebius of Samosata

The Greek Christian author Basil of Caesarea is usually remembered by church historians of late antiquity as an extremely important theologian, whose defense of the deity of the Holy Spirit in the final stages of the fourth-century Arian controversy played a critical role in the formulation of the orthodox Christian teaching about the Trinity. Basil has much to teach us, though, about other areas of the Christian life. Take, for instance, the vital area of Christian friendship.

Eusebius of Samosata: a brief sketch
One of Basil's closest friends was Eusebius, bishop of Samosata, a city on the Euphrates River, some 300 miles distant from Caesarea in Cappadocia. Samosata has been described by historian Lewis Ayres as a "strategically important city," for it was "close to the borders of the [Roman] Empire." Samosata contained Greek speakers like Eusebius, but also many Syriac- and Armenian-speaking Christians. Most of what we definitely know about Eusebius is from the letters of Basil. There is little doubt that the two men deeply enjoyed each other's presence and Basil delighted in having such a mentor.

His birth date is uncertain—Basil speaks of Eusebius' "venerable age" in his *Letter* 98, which would probably place his birth between 303 and 313 and this would mean he was probably a generation older than Basil. Their friendship thus cut across generational barriers. When he became the bishop of Samosata is also unclear. He was definitely in that position by 361.

Thirteen years later, in 374, by order of the Emperor Valens, who was an Arian (such people denied the full deity of the Lord Jesus), Eusebius was banished to Thrace in northern Greece. His congregation were devastated by the loss of their bishop. Some of them pursued Eusebius after he had been banished and, with tears, pled with him to stay with them and brave the wrath of the emperor. But Eusebius felt he had no choice but to obey the imperial order.

In 378, however, the persecuting policy of the emperor Valens was brought to a close by his death at the Battle of Adrianople in the Balkans. Valens' successor, the emperor Gratian, recalled a number of banished bishops, including Eusebius. But Eusebius was to enjoy his return to his congregation in Samosata for only two years. In 380 he travelled to Dolikha in northern Syria to participate in the ordination of a bishop for that city. An Arian woman took the opportunity to whip a tile at his head that proved to be fatal. It is noteworthy that, as he lay dying, Eusebius urged his followers to forgive the woman and not to harm her in any way.

Windows on his friendship with Basil

There are some fifteen extant letters of Basil to Eusebius that provide fascinating windows on their friendship. In the autumn of 368, Basil wrote to Eusebius informing him of his desire to visit him in Samosata so that he could enjoy Eusebius' "treasured wisdom" (*Letter* 27). A year later, Basil commended Eusebius for his zeal for the truth (*Letter* 34) and in 371 Basil told his friend that he hoped to see him the following spring so as "to be reinvigorated by your sound teaching" (*Letter* 48). Again, three years later Basil called Eusebius "the noble guardian of the faith, the faithful protector of the churches" (*Letter* 136). Friends are not afraid to point out areas of strength in those they love.

In a number of his letters to Eusebius, Basil also thanks his friend for his prayers: for church matters in which Basil is involved (*Letter* 30) and for Basil's health (*Letters* 100, 162). In August of 373, Basil's entire body was wracked with pain and he was deeply thankful Eusebius was remembering him in prayer. He told him that his letters were like "a beacon fire shining from afar upon the deep ... naturally possessing sweetness and great consolation" (*Letter* 100).

Basil used the imagery of sweetness again that year in *Letter* 138, when he told his friend that spending time with him the previous year, 372, had been like "a taste of very sweet honey." And again he urged the bishop of Samosata to pray for him. In one of Basil's final letters to Eusebius that we possess, *Letter* 241, written in 376—Basil died on January 1, 379—Basil again mentions Eusebius' praying. On this occasion, he likened his friend's prayers to those of Moses—high praise indeed.

Basil would have found it very odd that Christians can claim others as their friends and they not pray for them. If we say that we love one another and do not pray for each other, we lie and do not the truth.

10

We are all Augustinians:
reflecting on the legacy of Augustine

The Ancient Church gives us three great gifts: the doctrine of the Trinity, the canon of the New Testament, and the works of the African pastor-theologian Augustine. Some might be surprised to see the last in this list, but the truth of the matter is that we, who are heirs of western Christianity, are all Augustinians, so profound has been his influence. One gets an idea of his impact when one realizes that 95% of his written corpus survived his death when the Vandals, originally from Denmark, took the city of Hippo Regius at the time of his death in 430. Of his *City of God*, for instance, there are some 375 manuscript copies from late antiquity that can be used to establish the text of this work. So, what then is his theological legacy and how has he shaped us?

The Confessions
We know so much about Augustine because of his *Confessions*, which is actually one extended prayer of thanksgiving for the grace shown to him as a sinner by the Triune God. It establishes a new genre, that of the conversion narrative. One thus sees its influence in such works as John Bunyan's *Grace Abounding to the Chief of Sinners* and John Newton's *Authentic Narrative*. Through the account of his life, Augustine also establishes strongly a theology and spirituality of grace. Augustinian theology and piety are strongly shaped by a perspective that does full justice to human depravity and therefore the necessity of sovereign grace for conversion. This is developed at greater length in Augustine's treatises against Pelagius, who argued for the total freedom of the human will. This focus on the sovereignty of divine grace is fully present in his *Confessions*, but in a non-polemical form.

The *Confessions* also set forth a perspective on God that has had enormous influence on Western thought: God is a being of ultimate beauty. At the very onset of his Christian life, Augustine was deeply concerned about the question of beauty: what is it? What is its impact on the human frame? The *Confessions*, in a number of its prayers (see, for example,

31

Confessions 10.27), is Augustine's answer in part as it develops a vision of God that will enthrall Christians down to the close of the eighteenth century.

The Trinity

Augustine's second major work is *On the Trinity*, which clearly establishes the full deity of the Son and the Spirit from Scripture. Because the West by and large did not read Greek, Augustine's Trinitarianism was what was read and pondered down to the Reformation, and even beyond that to the close of the eighteenth century.

Most helpfully Augustine avoids modalism because of his emphasis on the eternal generation of the Son and the eternal generation of the Spirit. Sadly, the rediscovery of Trinitarian thought by evangelicals in the late twentieth century was not a return to Augustine, for eternal generation and eternal procession have been questioned and even rejected, and the distinction of persons found in the authority of the Father and so-called eternal submission of the Son. But this move fails to adequately distinguish the Spirit: how does his submission differ from that of the Son? And more importantly, this move separates the will of the Son from the will of the Father. But, if we look at the incarnation we see that will is tied to nature: there are two natures in the God-man Jesus of Nazareth and therefore two wills. But if we apply this to the Father's relationship with the Son, then we must have two divine natures, and thus at least two—and probably three—gods or tritheism. No: the Augustinian distinction of eternal generation and eternal procession is the only way to distinguish the persons.

Then, the Augustinian conception of the Spirit as the bond of love between the Father and the Son gives rise to (to name but three good examples of Augustinian influence): (a) the defence of the double procession of the Son and the Spirit from the Father by Anselm of Canterbury in the twelfth century; (b) the spirituality of Bernard of Clairvaux as found in his sermons on the Song of Songs; (c) and the Trinitarian thought of Jonathan Edwards in his *Essay on the Trinity*. This is a tremendous vision of the inner life of the Godhead: it is one ruled by love (note: the emphasis on the eternal submission of the Son presents us with a vision of God in which the keynote is power).

The City of God

Finally, Augustine's third major work *The City of God*, gives to the church a full-blown theology of history in which the Church, ruled by love for God and humility, runs its course through history as a pilgrim body. It also develops a very important way of reading culture and politics—through the lens of love. Cultures and political structures are defined by what they love.

To be sure, not all of Augustine's thought is helpful—one thinks of his view of human sexuality—but there is so much that is gold, that we should never be ashamed to own that our Christian Faith is profoundly Augustinian!

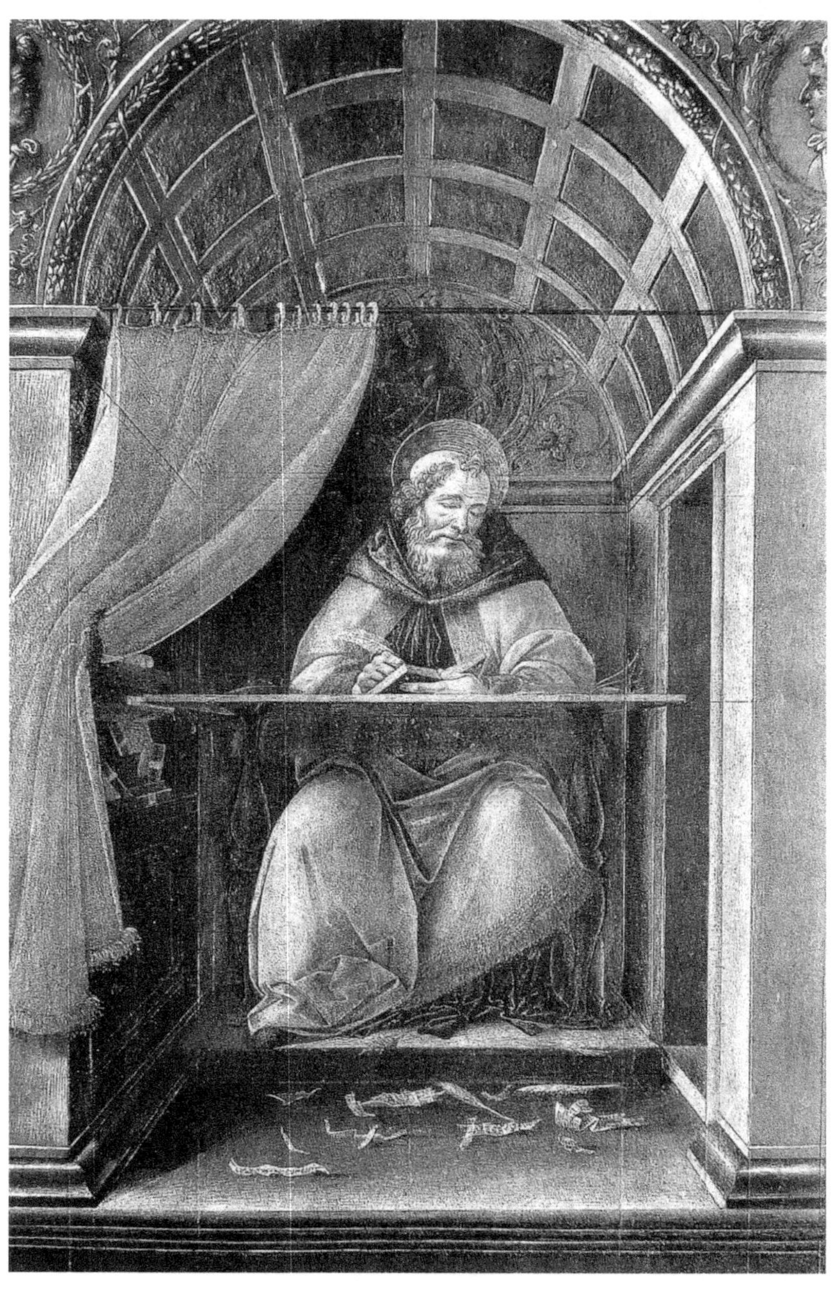

Augustine in his study (by Sandro Botticelli, 1494)

11

"Sacred Scripture ... is placed high on a throne": Augustine on the Bible

Augustine, like other Patristic authors, believed without hesitation that God had caused the Bible to be written. He accepted both its inspiration and its inerrancy. He thus used such terms as "inspire" (*inspirare*) and "dictate" (*dictare*) to stress that in the writing of Scripture the initiative is God's alone and that he determined what was to be written in the pages of Holy Writ. Augustine also consistently used the ablative case when referring to the work of the Holy Spirit in writing Scripture and the preposition "through" (*per*) when referring to the role of the biblical authors. By this means he made the same point: Scripture is wholly God's Word.

Honouring the canon

Where he encountered individual difficulties, he either suspended judgment or sought an explanation that would preserve biblical infallibility. Thus, he stated, "Only to those books which are called canonical have I learned to give honour so that I believe most firmly that no author in these books made any error in writing" (*Letter* 82.1.3).

Again, in his work against a Manichaean author named Faustus, Augustine emphasized that:

A distinction has been made between the books written after the apostles and the authentic canon of the Old and New Testament. Sacred Scripture ... is placed high on a throne where it receives the submission of all pious and faithful intelligence. There, if one finds something absurd, it is not permissible to say "The author of this book has strayed from the truth" but rather "This manuscript is false" or "The translator has made an error" or finally that "You do not grasp what is said" (*Against Faustus* 11.5).

His overall attitude to Scripture is well expressed by the following statement in a letter written to the Bible translator Jerome in 405:

I confess ... that ... I believe most firmly that only the authors [of the canonical books of Scripture] were completely free from error. And if in these writings I am perplexed by anything which appears to me contrary to the truth, I do not hesitate to suppose that either the manuscript is faulty, or the translator has not caught the meaning of what was said, or I myself have failed to understand it. But, when I read other authors, however eminent they may be in sanctity and learning, I do not necessarily believe a thing is true because they think so, but because they have been able to convince me, either on the authority of the canonical writers or by a probable reason which is not inconsistent with the truth (*Letter* 82.3).

A common persuasion

For Augustine, as for the rest of the early Christian authors, biblical inerrancy was a common persuasion. As Hans Küng, certainly no friend to biblical infallibility, has commented: for Augustine, "the whole Bible was free of contradictions, mistakes and errors." And the reason for this was pneumatological. Within two years of his conversion, in 388, Augustine could write that one must "be aware that everything in the Old as well as the New Testament has been written and entrusted by one Holy Spirit."

Last week, I noted that due to the pervasive influence of Augustine's thinking upon western Christianity, "we are all Augustinians" in one way or another. Would that all who profess faith in Christ would also follow him in this conviction that Scripture was to be "placed high on a throne" in the life of the Church!

12

Introducing Bede

If I were asked, which historian would I love to meet apart from the biblical authors, I would say without hesitation, Bede. An English Benedictine monk and scholar who lived in the late seventh and early eighth centuries, Bede is chiefly known for his *Church History of the English People* (*Historia Ecclesiastica Gentis Anglorum*), a history of England from the Roman occupation to 731, the year that it was completed. In the Middle Ages, though, Bede was equally known for his twenty or so commentaries on various books of the Bible and a work on the Lord's Prayer. In all, Bede wrote about 40 works, nearly all of which are extant. Regretfully, one that we do not have is his translation of the Gospel of John into Anglo-Saxon.

Bede's life

Bede lived through momentous times: the Byzantine empire and the Germanic kingdoms in western Europe were threatened by a vast pincer movement of the Muslim advance into the European continent. Two decisive battles saved Europe from Muslim conquest: in 718, when Bede was writing commentaries on the Scriptures, the Muslims were defeated before the walls of Constantinople; and in 732, but three years before his death, the Muslim army was defeated at Tours in France.

Despite such world-shaking events that were going on in his lifetime, his own life was relatively uneventful. He was born near Wearmouth, in northern Northumbria (now Sunderland, England), but we do not know the exact place nor the names of his parents, though he does indicate that he came from "noble stock." His parents had to have been Christians, but his grandparents were probably Anglo-Saxon pagans.

When he reached the age of seven, his parents took him to the monastery of Wearmouth and Jarrow to be raised as a monk—a common practice in the early Middle Ages. Remaining for the rest of his life in this monastery, he was ordained a deacon in 692/693, when he was nineteen, and later became a priest around 703, when he was in his thirtieth year.

He probably never went further south than York and no further north

37

than Lindisfarne. Bede never became an abbot, let alone bishop. He never met any rulers of state. "Even his holiness," in the words of the medievalist David Knowles, was "unobtrusive. He wrote of the wonders worked by others, but none are recorded of him. He described the conversion of England, but he probably never preached to anyone outside his monastery."

Bede as a scholar

The breadth of Bede's learning reveals the extensive library available to him and the level of culture achieved in England in his time. He was obviously fluent in Latin as well as his native Anglo-Saxon. And he also appears to have known Greek, which is quite remarkable, since knowledge of this language had been lost throughout most of western Europe. He himself has given us a good description of his literary studies: "I ever found it sweet to learn, or to teach, or to write."

He had little if any help in these pursuits, though. In the prologue to his commentary on Luke, Bede makes clear the difficulties under which he worked. He lacked the assistance of amanuenses and librarians, and his studies had to be fitted into the hours left over after he completed his many monastic chores. As he said: "I am my own secretary, I make my own notes. I am my own librarian."

It is thus amazing that one hundred years after the mission of Augustine of Canterbury to evangelize the Anglos-Saxons, the Anglo-Saxon Church contained a man who was the most learned scholar in Western Europe. In his *Paradiso*, Dante placed Bede among the twelve most leaned "men through whom the Word of God was mediated in wisdom to the world."

13

Bede as a model historian

The Anglo-Saxon historian Bede is best known for his *Church History of the English People*, as we noted last week. Why does this historical work—which traces the history of England from the Roman occupation to 731, the year that it was completed, as well as detailing the conversion of the Anglo-Saxon peoples—merit calling Bede a model historian?

A providential reading of history

Well, two reasons stand out. First of all, Bede read history providentially. In his view, God was at work in history. He saw his work in this regard as a continuation of what Luke the historian did in the Book of Acts.

Theologically, Bede was also deeply indebted to the theology of Augustine, the North African theologian of late antiquity. As such, he believed firmly in the sovereignty of God in both the universe and human life. History, therefore, was not simply a record of the doings of men and women, kings and commoners. It recorded also the doings of God.

Of course, we may disagree with the way that he read history. Bede was deeply concerned to stress the unity of the Church throughout Western Europe and thus he was quite critical of the Celtic Church that was in the British Isles when the mission of Augustine of Canterbury arrived in what later would become Kent. On two occasions Augustine met with some Welsh representatives of the churches in Wales and the meetings did not go well at all. Bede blamed the Welsh and he felt justified in doing so, because after these failed meetings, a number of these Welsh Christians from Bangor were killed at a battle that took place at Chester, thus indicating God's displeasure with them (*Church History* 2.2).

While I personally think Bede read this historical incident wrongly, it would be a mistake to conclude that we should never read history providentially.

A storyteller

Then, second, one of the key reasons why Bede's *Church History of the*

39

English People has stood the test of time is because he is such a great story-teller. History is filled with tremendous stories and Bede had a marvelous ear and pen for such. For example, when the Christian Faith came to the kingdom of Northumbria, the pagan king, Edwin, hesitated to accept it. He asked for advice from his senior counsellors (*ealdormen* in Anglo-Saxon), and one of them, according to Bede, said this:

> The present life of man, O king, seems to me, in comparison of that time which is unknown to us, to be like the swift flight of a sparrow through the hall in which you sit at supper in winter with your ealdormen and thanes. A good fire is burning on the hearth in the middle of the hall and all inside is warm, while outside the wintry storms of rain and snow are raging. The sparrow flies in one door and quickly out at the other. While he is within the hall, he is safe from the wintry storm; but after the briefest space of calm, he immediately vanishes out of your sight into the dark winter from which he had emerged. So, this life of man appears for a short space, but of what went before or what is to follow, we are utterly ignorant. If, therefore, this new doctrine contains something more certain, it seems right for us to follow it (*Church History* 2.13).

It is a great scene. There is the huge royal hall, so typical of Anglo-Saxon kingdoms (think of the hall of Théoden of Rohan in *The Lord of the Rings*) and the fire on the hearth in the depths of winter. Outside it is grey and cold and freezing but inside warm and toasty. For a moment the sparrow appears and then is gone, back into the cold and dark. What a vivid picture of pagan hopelessness before the light of the Gospel came to Northumbria.

14

John of Damascus and
an early Christian response to Islam

The last twenty years or so have thrust to the fore of Evangelical consciousness our great need to share the gospel with Muslims. But Christian concern about the salvation of those devoted to the teachings of Muhammad is nothing new, though many Evangelicals have little or no memory of the long history of Christianity's interaction with Islam. One ancient vista from which to see the way that Christians responded to Islam during the very earliest period of Muslim expansion in the seventh and eight centuries are the writings of the theologian John of Damascus, who died around 750. John had clearly taken the time to understand Islamic views and thinking, and was quite familiar with the Qur'ān in Arabic, though his language about Islam could at times be somewhat intemperate.

A biographical sketch

John is often described as the last of the so-called Church Fathers of the Ancient Church. An Arab by ethnicity, his grandfather had played a key role in the surrender of Damascus in 635 to the Muslim army of Khalid ibn al-Walid, probably the greatest of early Muslim generals. The Muslim rulers of Syria were tolerant of the presence of Christians and John's grandfather became a key administrator in the Muslim government of the region. John's father, Ibn Mansur, was known as an extremely devout Christian but also one of the most trusted officials in the Muslim regime.

John succeeded his father as a key advisor to the Muslim ruler, Caliph Abd al-Malik. After a long life of service in the public realm John left his position early in the eighth century in order to embrace a monastic lifestyle in a monastery near Jerusalem. John was a prolific writer and among his writings there are two that specifically address Islam: *On Heresies*, a work that catalogues various heresies that had and were afflicting the Church—chapter 101 is devoted especially to Islam—and *A Dialogue Between a Saracen and a Christian.*

Identifying key differences between Islam and Christianity
In *On Heresies* 101 John locates Muhammad historically and then identifies some of his key theological teachings. According to John, Muhammad asserts that "there is one God" and that "Christ is the Word of God and His Spirit, only a creation and servant, and that he was born without seed from Mary, the sister of Moses and Aaron." John also notes that according to Muhammad, "Christ … was not crucified nor did he die, for God took him to himself into heaven because he loved him," an accurate rendition of what is said in Qur'ãn 4.157. Obviously, this assertion strikes at the heart of biblical Christianity in which the death of Christ for sinners is absolutely central for their salvation.

After mentioning the fact that the revelation of Muhammad, though it claims to be in succession to the Old and New Testaments, was not foretold by these earlier witnesses, John proceeds to deal with the Muslim critique of the Trinity: "they call us *Associaters*, because, they say, we introduce an associate to God by saying Christ is the Son of God and God." John is responding here to a fierce monotheistic declaration like this—one of many in the Qu'rãn:

> People of the Book, do … not say anything about God except the truth: the Messiah, Jesus, son of Mary, was nothing more than a messenger of God … So believe in God and His messengers and do not speak of a 'Trinity' … God is only one God, He is far above having a son (4.171).

John's response must ultimately be our response: the teaching of the deity of Christ, and the Trinity, is what is found in the Scripture. Though the doctrine of the Trinity is indeed difficult to comprehend, it is biblical truth. As John writes about the triumph of Christianity in the Roman Empire in another work, *The Orthodox Faith*:

> Altars and temples of idols have been overthrown. Knowledge of God has been implanted. The consubstantial Trinity, the uncreated Godhead is worshipped … Hope of the resurrection has been granted through the resurrection of Christ. … Yes, and most wonderful of all is that all these things were successfully brought about through a cross and suffering and death. The gospel of the

knowledge of God has been preached to the whole world and has put the adversaries to flight not by war and arms and camps. Rather, it was a few unarmed, poor, unlettered, persecuted, tormented, done-to-death men, who, by preaching One who had died and was crucified in the flesh, prevailed over the wise and powerful, because the almighty power of the Crucified was with them.

As was the triumph of the gospel then, may it be so again, and that among the followers of Muhammad!

15

Word or image?
Wisdom from Theodulf of Orléans

The *Caroline Books* were drawn up by Theodulf of Orléans—one of the key theologians of the Carolingian church and the author of the well-known hymn "All glory, laud, and honour"—in 790–793 and then later revised by him with the help of, among others, Alcuin of York, the private tutor to Charlemagne and the head of the palace school at Aachen. It was a well-argued response by the Latin-speaking Carolingian Church to what are known as the iconodulist decrees of the Second Council of Nicaea (787). In essence, the *Libri Carolini* sought to refute this council's advocacy of the use of icons as vehicles of worship and that such icons deserved the identical adoration as due to God. In light of recent discussions about worship and the so-called contemporary inability to primarily use words—notably the sermon—as a vehicle for worship, it has some interesting observations to add to these discussions.

Theodulf was a Visigothic churchman who was deeply influenced by the writings of Augustine, particularly the latter's *On Christian Teaching*. This Augustinian work, which deals broadly with hermeneutics and was often treated as a manual for preachers in the early Middle Ages, provided Theodulf with the resources to argue that the Bible alone is, in the words of Celia Chazelle, "the material object to which the Christian can turn to gain knowledge of the spiritual realm, because it was granted by God for this purpose." Augustine was fairly severe on artistic representation. He argued that it was a "useless institution" that the serious student of Scripture needed to avoid. Relying on this Augustinian work, Theodulf was thus convinced that the Greek Orthodox advocacy of icons was due to their poor understanding of the beauty and riches of Scripture. The latter has all that a believer needs.

Celia Chazelle notes that Theodulf's critique is also tied up with "the concept that writing in general has greater merit as an instrument of communication than does artistic depiction." A picture, since it is material, does not partake of the spiritual realm. By definition, it must resemble that to which it refers and thus it cannot really inform its viewers about the realm of the Spirit. Words, on the other hand, are not so limited, for words are signs that do not have to resemble their subjects. And going along with this powerful advocacy of the written word and the supremacy of Scripture was an attempt to make Carolingian society an increasingly literate culture.

Summing up the thrust of the argument of the *Caroline Books* and its similarity to Augustine's *On Christian Teaching*, Chazelle states:

> Both treatises insist on the supremacy of words as signs over all other forms of communication accessible to humans; both stress the difficulty, subtlety, and richness of written language, especially Scripture, and both maintain that the Christian who does not investigate the Bible's language carefully or with sufficient grasp of the rules governing written language runs the danger of misinterpreting Scripture's message. Both treatises make it clear that interest in artistic representations is incompatible with study of the Bible.

There is much wisdom here and again a good reminder that there is nothing new under the sun.

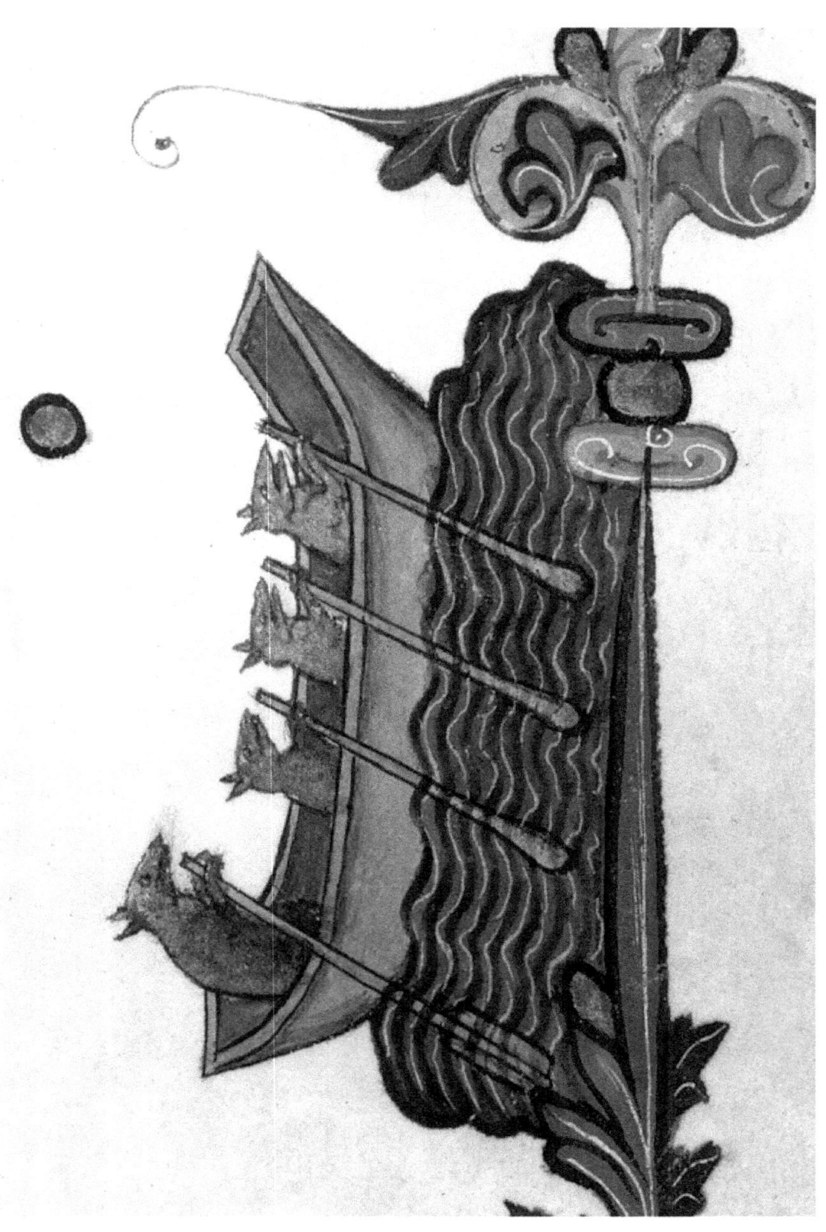

A whimsical medieval depiction of four rats rowing a boat

16

The church and the bubonic plague
in the late Middle Ages

As historians look at history, they seek to discern the forces or people that have shaped the past. My own historical convictions have led me to focus on people as the main actors on the stage of history, not economic force or ideologies per se. Yet, there is definitely a place to evaluate the impact of such forces as these or that of pandemics.

For instance, consider the impact of pestilence on the forces of the Athenian Empire during the early stages of the Peloponnesian War with Sparta and her allies, a war made famous by the Greek historian Thucydides. The loss of the Athenian general Pericles to this plague may well have affected Athenian fortunes in that war. The conquest of the Aztec world by the Spaniard Hernán Cortés was largely facilitated by a smallpox epidemic that the Spanish conquerors brought with them and against which the Aztecs had no natural immunity.

The bubonic plague
Understandably, the church has not been unaffected by various epidemics/pandemics down through the years. In the fourteenth century, for instance, Europe experienced the devastation of the bubonic plague, which first reached Europe in 1348, and which carried away at least one third and possibly as many as forty percent of the entire European population (which was around 25 million at the time). Episodes of the plague reoccurred down to the seventeenth century: in the fourteenth and fifteenth centuries alone there were recorded outbreaks in 1362, 1368, 1374, 1381, 1390, 1399, 1405, 1410, 1423, and 1429.

In the medieval era, this pestilence was rooted in the unsanitary conditions of the Middle Ages, which have been described as "a thousand years without a bath!" The bubonic plague—or Black Death as it came to be known—was caused by the bacillus *Pasteurella pestis*, which likes to live in the stomachs of those fleas that reside in the hair of rodents, sometimes a squirrel, but preferably the black rat (*rattus rattus*). These rats usually make their homes close to human habitations and in this way those rats that were infected became spreaders of the plague. The initial wave of the plague may well have been caused by rats on board the ships of knights returning from fighting the Muslims in Palestine.

The bubonic plague was so-called since it produced swollen lymph nodes, or "buboes." When it spread to the lungs, it produced the less common, but deadlier, pneumonic plague. The latter is caught by inhaling infected respiratory droplets from people who are sick. Today, it is easily curable with antibiotics if treated within 24 hours of its onset.

The church responds

What was the impact of this medieval plague on the Church? Well, first of all there was an exacerbation of anti-semitism. Since Jewish ghettoes in western European cities tended to be more sanitary environments due to the observance of the cleanliness laws of the Old Testament, Jewish deaths from the bubonic plague were fewer. But this only convinced their fellow Europeans that they were poisoning the wells of the Christians and led to a distinct rise in anti-Semitic sentiments.

A distinct uptick in Marian devotion is also traceable to this era, since it was commonly believed that Mary played a critical role in convincing her Son to end the plague in the course of the fourteenth century. Trust in Mary's saving power increasingly became a key element of late medieval spirituality. In time this devotion to Mary would lead to the addition of the clause "Holy Mary, Mother of God, pray for us sinners now, and at the hour of our death" by the fifteenth-century preacher Girolamo Savonarola to the prayer known as the *Ave Maria* ("Hail Mary").

Finally, the artistic portrayal of the death of Christ became much more realistic—and gruesome. Portrayals of the crucified Christ prior to the advent of the bubonic plague usually displayed Christ reigning from the cross, crowned and fully clothed. Such portrayals were not at all realistic. But after the waves of the bubonic plague in the fourteenth century, Christ's death was portrayed in all of its physical horror, and meditation on his physical sufferings became a key part of medieval piety.

In other words, some of the key elements that disturbed the Reformers about medieval piety are traceable to this era. How should the church have responded? In a few weeks, we shall consider one possible answer in the response of the Puritans to a wave of the bubonic plague that hit London in 1665.

17

Why we still need to remember the Reformation

One of the good gifts that God has given to human beings is that of memory and the facility to remember the past. Remembering our own personal past is absolutely vital to knowing who we are and having a sense of personal identity. We all know how diseases that ravage a person's memory destroy the ability of that person to function in any meaningful way in the present. The same holds true for communities and nations. When a community or nation forgets its past and where it has come from, it finds itself completely disoriented and ultimately unable to move ahead into the future. Of course, like any good gift in our fallen world, this gift of remembering can be abused. It can bind a person, and even a community, to the past in hopeless regret or unforgiving bitterness or even vengeful hatred.

But if it is true that knowledge of the past is vital to meaningful living in the present and the future, and I believe it is, then Evangelicals in the West face a very uncertain future for we are living in a day when knowledge of our past as Evangelical Christians is abysmally low. Who were our forebears and what did they believe? What was their experience of God and how did that shape the churches they founded, churches which we have inherited? Far too many Western Evangelicals neither know nor do they care. In this regard, they are actually indistinguishable from Western culture, which is passionately in love with the present, eagerly anticipating the future, and totally disinterested in the past, or if nodding interest is shown in the past it is used as a vehicle for escapist entertainment. There is no serious grappling with the past to derive wisdom for the present or future. Evangelical forgetfulness of the past is thus actually a species of worldliness.

The vital importance of remembering
The Scriptures, on the other hand, make much of remembering:

- Deuteronomy 24:9: "Remember what the LORD your God did to Miriam on the way as you came out of Egypt."

53

- 1 Chronicles 16:12/Psalm 105:5: "Remember the wondrous works that he [that is, the Lord] has done, his miracles and the judgments he uttered.
- Luke 17:32: "Remember Lot's wife."
- Hebrews 13:7: "Remember your leaders, those who spoke to you the word of God. Consider the outcome of their way of life, and imitate their faith." Note that this call to remembrance comes after the longest chapter in Hebrews, chapter 11, where God's heroes of faith are remembered.

Remembering the Reformation

Over the next few weeks, we will take time to remember key aspects from that movement of revival and reform that we call the Reformation, which initiated by Martin Luther nailing the 95 Theses to the church door in Wittenberg in Germany. We do so because the events of the Reformation have given rise to the host of Evangelical churches that exist today. If the events of those revolutionary years had not happened things would be quite different today. We are going to remember that era not only to gain a better idea of where we have come from, but also because people from that day can give us wisdom and guidance in the present.

Three important questions

Speaking concisely, the Reformation was necessary because far too much of the Church during the Middle Ages had forgotten the answers to three very important questions:

- What saves a person from judgment and hell?
- Who saves us from judgment and hell?
- How do we know the answers to these two questions?

In the next few weeks, we shall revisit the glorious answers that the Reformation gave to these vital questions.

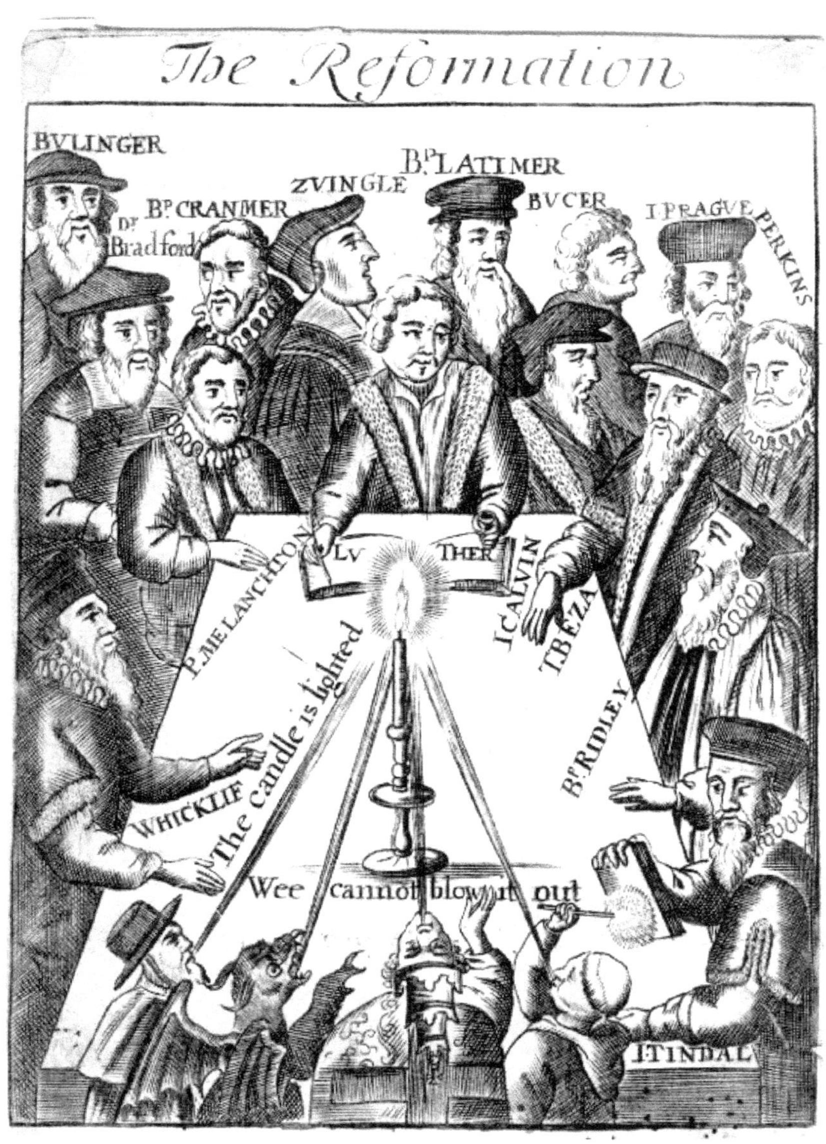

"The Candlestick": A famous depiction of the Reformation as a lit candle surrounded by a number of prominent Reformers with four figures at the foot of the picture (including the Pope) attempting to extinguish the light of the candle

18

The egg-laying of Erasmus: the first published Greek New Testament

"The name of Erasmus will never perish." This comment in a 1516 letter by John Colet, one of Erasmus' scholarly friends, says much about the way that Erasmus was viewed by many in his day: he was, without doubt, the most famous scholar of his time. The illegitimate son of a priest, Erasmus was born at Gouda in the Netherlands between 1465 and 1469. His early education was with the Brethren of the Common Life, a semi-monastic movement of lay people founded in the Netherlands by Gerard Groote. Erasmus studied in this communal context for eleven years or so and it was here that he began his study of Greek that would lead to his fame later in life.

In 1492, he was ordained a priest in the Roman Church. It is vital to note that although he would be eventually condemned by Rome as a heretic, he strove to remain a faithful member of this church body. As he mentioned in a letter to Alberto Pio III, the Italian Prince of Carpi, written on October 10, 1525: the "Lutherans alternately courted me and menaced me. For all this, I did not move a finger's breadth from the teaching of the Roman Church."

Erasmus was deeply concerned about the rampant immorality and corruption in the church in western Europe. A good window on his view of the needed church reforms can be found in *The Handbook of the Christian Soldier* (1501). For Erasmus, true Christianity consists not of doctrinal rectitude, but of the inward love of God and neighbor. This is Erasmus' master thought: the Christian life is primarily one of imitation. As he wrote in this work: "You venerate saints; you are glad to touch their relics. But you condemn what good they have left, namely the example of a pure life. No worship of Mary is more gracious than if you imitate Mary's humility."

Publishing the Greek New Testament

Erasmus did not realize that Roman Church needed more drastic medicine, though. Her doctrinal foundations needed a major overhaul. In that regard, Erasmus' greatest work, his publication of the Greek New Testament in March 1516, would play a significant role.

The first printing press had appeared in the mid-1450s, but it took fifty years or so for a European publishing house to commit to the publication of the Greek New Testament. One reason for this was the fact that the production of metal Greek letters was both difficult and expensive. The principal reason, though, had to do with the prestige enjoyed by the Latin Bible of the Middle Ages. Since it was regarded as an inspired text, what need was there for a copy of the Greek New Testament or the Hebrew Old Testament?

The first plans for the publishing of the Greek New Testament were developed by Cardinal Francisco Ximenes de Cizners, the primate of Spain. He envisioned an edition that combined Hebrew, Aramaic, Greek, and Latin. It was printed at Complutum (now Alcalá), Spain—hence the name by which it has become known to historians, the Complutensian Polyglot. The New Testament of this edition was actually printed by 1514, though it was not published till 1522. The first published Greek New Testament was that of Erasmus.

Erasmus' egg-laying

In August 1514, Johann Froben, a Swiss publisher in Basle, approached Erasmus about the possibility of his supervising an edition of the Greek New Testament. Undoubtedly Froben had heard of the forthcoming Spanish Bible, and being the smart businessman he was, he sensed that the market was ready for an edition of the Greek New Testament and that there was a tremendous opportunity to make money on such a publication. Erasmus was not able to begin serious work on this edition until the summer of 1515.

At the heart of his edition were two twelfth-century manuscripts from a monastic library in Basle. In all, he used five manuscripts (today, we have more than six thousand manuscripts). There was also the weakness of his manuscript resources (his copy of Revelation, for example, lacked the final six verses of the book and Erasmus had to back-translate from his Latin Bible into Greek to acquire the Greek of these verses!). Printing began in September or October, 1515, and was completed in March, 1516. The weakness of his manuscript base and the haste with which the text was produced (hastiness was a weakness of Erasmus and he hated proofreading his own work) all but ensured that the 1516 publication would have numerous typos. It would eventually be superseded as New Testament scholarship developed, though this would not actually take place until the nineteenth century. Later editions of Erasmus' Greek New Testament (in 1519, 1522, 1527, and 1535) exercised enormous influence. Martin Luther used the second edition for his definitive German translation and William Tyndale's fabulous English translation was based on the third edition of 1522.

Erasmus had longed to see the medieval church reformed. In the providence of God his Greek New Testament would be critical in the reformation needed. No wonder some Franciscan monks in Cologne twitted, "Erasmus laid the egg and Luther hatched it"!

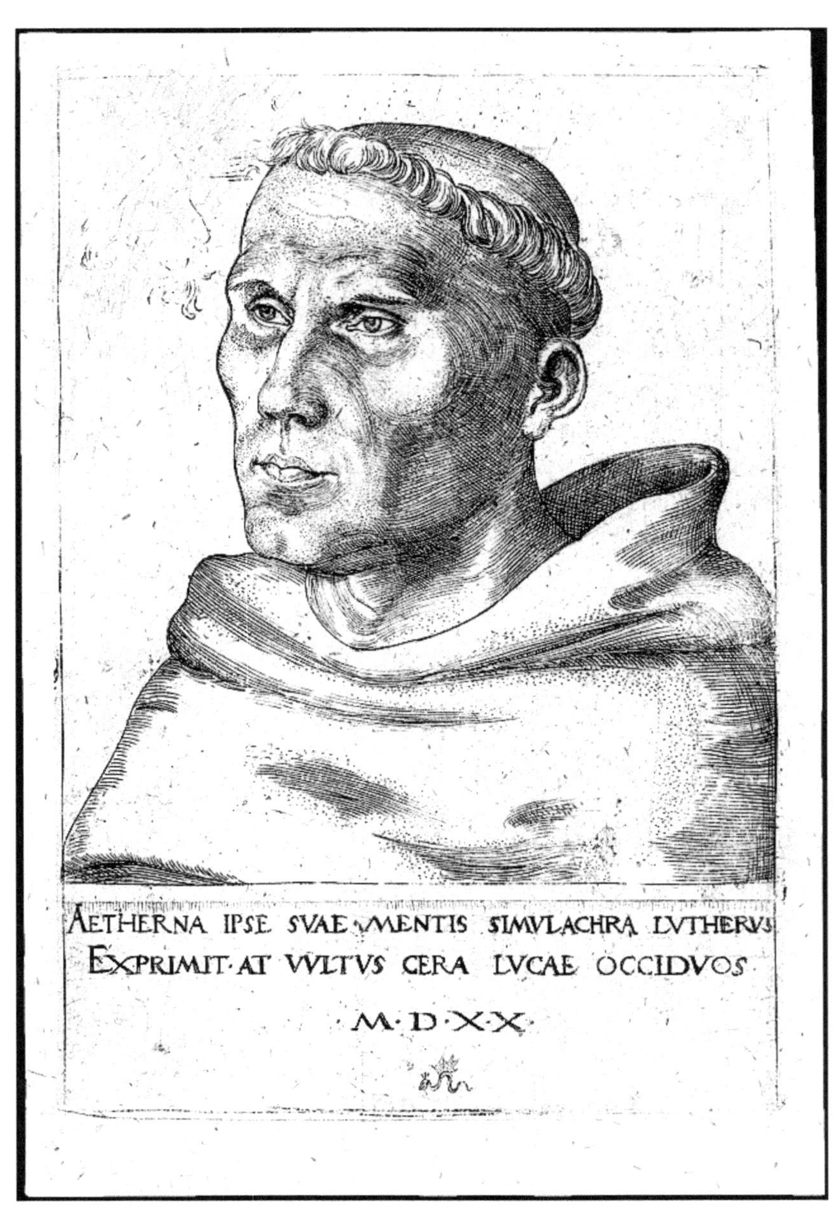

Martin Luther

19

Revival at Heidelberg, 1518

By nature, Martin Luther was not a rebel. The protest that has come to be called the *95 Theses* took him along a pathway he never envisioned when he first put pen to paper. What began as a simple critique of the misguided piety of the Roman Church ended in taking Luther and his colleagues at the University of Wittenberg to the remarkable place of forming a new church, or, as Luther would have put it, guiding the church back to its biblical foundations.

The *95 Theses* were designed to initiate a theological conversation. They worked far better than their author imagined! And in the year following their publication, Luther was asked to speak about his theological convictions at what has come to be called the Heidelberg Disputation. It bears remembering that when Luther burst onto the stage of history in this debate he had a deep knowledge of Latin literature and was firmly acquainted with both scholastic philosophy and theology, as well as with the writings of the Renaissance humanists of his own day. Most importantly he was deeply read in the Latin Fathers and had a profound knowledge of the Bible.

Luther's 28 theses at the Heidelberg Disputation
In April of 1518, Luther walked some 350 miles to give an account of his views to various papal representatives at Heidelberg in the Palatinate. His spiritual mentor Johann Staupitz had urged him to be non-controversial, which meant saying nothing about the practice of indulgences. Luther appears to have followed his advice, for the 28 theses he presented for discussion say nothing about indulgences, which had formed a major subject in the earlier *95 Theses*.

At the outset, Luther stressed that he was reliant upon the thought of "St. Paul, the especially chosen vessel and instrument of Christ, and also from St. Augustine, his most trustworthy interpreter." He began by maintaining that God's Law, though it was "the most salutary doctrine of life, cannot advance man on his way to righteousness, but rather hinders him" (thesis 1). Face to face with the Law, human beings are accused of their sin, judged and condemned (thesis 23).

Moreover, the darling of humanity, free will, is actually a fiction and can never, without grace, lead to righteous deeds (theses 13–15). Thus, "the person who believes that he can obtain grace by doing what is in him adds sin to sin so that he becomes doubly guilty" (thesis 16). Lest some think this a recipe for despair, Luther rightly reasoned that that this should push sinners to humble themselves and "seek the grace of Christ" (thesis 18). Thus, Luther concluded: "He is not righteous who does much, but he who, without work, believes much in Christ" (thesis 25).

Three of the theses—numbers 19–21—deal with the nature of the true theologian. The latter is one who makes the crucified Christ and suffering foundational to his understanding of life (thesis 20). Such a "theologian of the cross" sees the world as it really is, knowing that without the cross we are nothing and all our works mere vanity (thesis 21).

Revival at Heidelberg

One of those present at this theological conference was Martin Bucer, who later led the reformation in Strasbourg and whose latter years were spent teaching in Cambridge. His view of Luther's conduct at the debate bears quoting at length:

> Although our chief men contradicted him with all their might, their wiles were not able to make him move one inch from his propositions. His sweetness in answering is remarkable, his patience in listening is incomparable … his answers, so brief, so wise, and drawn from the Holy Scriptures, easily made all his hearers his admirers. On the next day I had a familiar and friendly conference with the man alone and a supper rich with doctrine rather than with dainties.

The net result was that almost the entire German contingent of Luther's monastic order, the Augustinians, went over to Luther's views!

As Jeremy Jackson rightly noted in his history of the church, we often forget the nature of the Reformation as a great spiritual revival. We identify the Reformation simply with the reforming of doctrine. But there would have been no Reformation unless it had been accompanied by the Spirit's reviving work of regeneration and conversion. The impact of Luther's preaching at the Heidelberg Disputation 500 years ago is nothing less than a tremendous illustration of this truth.

20

Solo Sancto Spiritu: Luther at Worms in 1521

On April 18, 1521, Martin Luther experienced what was probably the most dangerous moment of the entirety of his life. He had been asked to appear before the Holy Roman Emperor, the Spaniard Charles V, at the imperial parliament (diet) which had been called to meet at Worms, which was situated on the Upper Rhine, about forty miles south of Frankfurt.

Luther's teaching

In the previous four years there had been a number of attempts by key authorities in the Roman Church to convince Luther of the errors of his teaching that Christians are declared righteous by a holy God simply by faith alone in the crucified Christ (see Week 22). It was rightly understood by all who took part in the ensuing controversy that Luther's views rendered much of the medieval system of piety utterly worthless. Charles had been given the authority to burn Luther at the stake if he refused to recant.

Luther first appeared before the emperor on April 17. It would have to have been an awe-inspiring occasion with all of the German princes and nobles and their retinues as well as the emperor and his Spanish guard. Luther was presented with the thirty or so books he had written since 1517 and asked if he would renounce them.

It was an unusually diffident Luther who replied. He asked for twenty-fours to consider his reply. This was granted and he appeared before Charles V again the following day, April 18. When asked the same question as the day before, Luther's diffidence was gone, swept away by what was his usual boldness.

Luther's response to the emperor

He told the emperor that his books fell into three categories: there were books of piety, like his marvellous *The Freedom of a Christian* (1520), and of course, he felt there was nothing wrong in those and how could he reject their teachings. Then there were those books in which he had criticized the papacy, and there was no way he was going to recant from such attacks,

65

because the pope was wrong in maintaining views at odds with a plain reading of Scripture. And then there were books responding to those who had critiqued his attacks on the bishop of Rome. Again, he was not prepared to recant from anything in those, since they should not have defended such blatant errors, though he was sorry for the harshness of the tone of his attacks.

He then declared in words that have echoed down to the present-day, "Unless I am convinced by the testimony of the Scriptures or by clear reason (for I do not trust either in the pope or in councils alone, since it is well known that they have often erred and contradicted themselves), I am bound by the Scriptures I have quoted and my conscience is captive to the Word of God. I cannot and will not recant anything, since it is neither safe nor right to go against conscience. May God help me. Amen."

The significance of Luther's words
Luther's brave stand at Worms, face to face most likely with a fiery death, sealed the break with Rome of those who came to be called Protestants. It also decisively determined that the movement that followed in his train—Lutheran, Reformed, Anglican, and even Anabaptist—would be a biblicistic one in which a spirituality of the Word shaped its piety. And though the Reformers did not realize it in their day, Luther standing before the most powerful prince in Europe with the Scriptures as his only armament set the tone for the church in the far future, when she cast the support of princes to the four winds and relied solely upon the Holy Spirit—*solo Sancto Spiritu*, "by the Holy Spirit alone."

21

To spite the Pope:
Martin Luther on marriage as paradisiacal

From the point of view of the opponents of the Reformation, one of its most scandalous aspects was its reinterpretation of the spirituality of marriage. The standard line during the long medieval era had been that a robust Christian life could only be found in a state of celibacy. The early medieval author Bede, whom we looked at a few weeks ago, expressed this conviction when he maintained that the apostolic injunction to pray always could not be fulfilled if one was married and engaging in sexually intimate acts. Sex precluded a robust prayer life.

Not surprisingly the requirement of celibacy for vocational ministry led to an unbearable burden in the lives of many medieval priests, monks and nuns. Far too many of them were celibate but not chaste. The Reformation solution to this scandal of sexual immorality was to go back to the Scriptures and recover a truly biblical view of marriage.

Luther's 1519 sermon on marriage
Even before Martin Luther's 1525 marriage to Katharina von Bora, for instance, he had given serious thought to the meaning of marriage. In a 1519 sermon, he noted that "a woman is created to be a companionable help-meet to the man in everything." In other words, for most people, marriage was vital to true godliness. Indeed, Luther went on to note, "the love of a man and woman is (or should be) the greatest and purest of all loves." In fact, Luther asserted, if Adam and Eve had not fallen, this love would have been "the loveliest thing."

As it is, though, the fall has deeply tainted marriage and human thinking about this divine institution, and for many it had become simply a context to give rein to "the lust of the flesh." Medieval church authorities had used this as a key reason to urge people to embrace celibacy. Luther, and the Reformers in general, did the opposite.

Luther urged men and women to marry, but to recognize the great goal of human sexuality: the procreation of children. As he noted in this sermon, the bearing and raising of children was a much greater work than "all the pilgrimages to Rome, Jerusalem, or Compostella [in Spain]" or the building of churches.

A letter on marriage

Two years later one of Luther's friends, the humanist Nikolaus Gerbel, who was a lawyer in Strasbourg and who died in 1560, got married and Luther wrote to congratulate him on November 1, 1521. It is not known how the two men had met but it is clear that by this point in time they had a fast friendship. Luther was happy for Gerbel's marriage, for by it the lawyer had escaped from the evils of the medieval perspective on celibacy. In fact, Luther went on, "I am daily gaining more insight into the godless lives of the unmarried of both sexes, so that nothing sounds worse to me than the words monk, nun, priest, for I regard a married life of deep poverty as paradise in comparison."

The medieval church had long supposed that the celibate life of a monk or nun was the nearest thing to the paradisiacal experience of the angels. Not as far as Luther was concerned! In fact, the temptations to which the unmarried were exposed revealed the godlessness of the Roman church more than anything else since it dictated celibacy for those called to ministry and ardently promoted such. As Johannes Bugenhagen, Luther's own pastor in Wittenberg, put it, "It is faith, and not virginity, that fills paradise."

Luther's own marriage

Luther himself married in June of 1525. A group of nuns had escaped from a nunnery in the town of Grimma and gotten to Wittenberg, where Luther found himself acting as a marriage broker. By 1525 all of them had found husbands except for one, Katherina von Bora, who had set her cap for Luther. They were married on June 13, 1525. When asked why he had married an ex-nun, Luther replied that it was to spite the Pope! This impish remark has its roots, of course, in Luther's analysis of medieval monasticism and his determination to retrieve a truly biblical view of marriage.

22
The Reformers divided

At the time of the Reformation there was a great division in the ranks of the Reformers over an issue of spirituality. It concerned one of the means of grace, namely the Lord's Supper. While all of the Reformers clearly rejected the Roman Catholic dogma of transubstantiation and the superstitions that had arisen with it, they were deeply divided over the answer to the question, "How is Christ present at the Table?"

Differing views of Luther and Zwingli
In the view of Martin Luther, Christ's body and blood are present "in, with and under" the bread and the wine. Just as when an iron poker is placed within the flaming fire of a forge, it becomes red-hot if left in the fire long enough, so do the bread and the wine actually contain Christ's body after the prayer of consecration. Contrary to the Roman dogma of transubstantiation, the bread remains bread and the wine remains wine. But they now contain the body and blood of Christ.

The Swiss Reformer Huldreich Zwingli, on the other hand, regarded the bread and the wine as mainly signs of what God has accomplished through the death of Christ and the Supper therefore as chiefly a memorial. In recent discussions of Zwingli's perspective on the Lord's Supper it is often maintained that Zwingli was not really a Zwinglian, that is, he saw more in the Lord's Supper than simply a memorial. Be this as it may, a tradition did take its start from those aspects of his thought that stressed primarily the memorial nature of the Lord's Supper.

A failed attempt at reconciliation
The German ruler Philip of Hesse, who had embraced the convictions of the Reformation, was deeply concerned that such a division among the Reformers would jeopardize the political future of the Reformation. He was concerned that Roman Catholic princes would seek to exploit this division to politically roll back the advance of the Reformation. Philip thus arranged for a colloquy to take place at Marburg in the fall of 1529 that would heal

this division between the two Reformation giants, Luther and Zwingli.

Luther, it needs to be noted, went unwillingly to the meeting, though Zwingli was eager to end their division. On the first day of the conference, October 1, Hesse arranged for Luther's co-worker, Philipp Melanchthon to meet with Zwingli, and for the Swiss Reformer Johann Oecolampadius to confer with Luther. The following day Zwingli and Luther met. It was an explosive meeting that failed to unite the two Christian leaders. Luther insisted that "this is my body" means simply that: the word "is" needs to be taken literally—the bread is the body of Christ. Zwingli, convinced that the risen body of Christ had ascended to heaven and could not be literally present in every locale where the Lord's Supper was being celebrated, insisted as vehemently that the elements must therefore be symbols that were designed to prompt remembrance.

The legacy of division

Luther refused to recognize the Swiss Reformer as a genuine Christian and thus their division remained unhealed. And as Philip of Hesse had feared, Roman Catholic princes took advantage of this division. Two years later, in October of 1531, some 7,000 Roman Catholic soldiers attacked the canton of Zurich. Zwingli marched out to meet them at Kappel, where he and around 500 other Protestants were killed in battle. The Roman Catholic troops had been confident that the German Lutheran princes would not support Zwingli, and thus the boldness of their attack on Zurich.

The division between these two German-speaking Reformers and its sad legacy is a sobering reminder of the danger of dividing over issues that cannot be biblically demonstrated as being primary. When facing Christian division, we all still need to pray the prayer that Zwingli uttered before the Colloquy of Marburg: "Fill us, O Lord and Father of us all, we beseech Thee, with thy gentle Spirit, and dispel on both sides all the clouds of misunderstanding and passion."

23

The emergence of the Anabaptists

One of the legacies of the Reformation is the emergence of two main religious groups in Western Europe claiming to be Christian, the Roman Catholics and the Protestants. And though they disagreed with each other on certain key matters that we have already noted in previous weeks—issues like the nature of salvation and the question of religious authority—it is important to recognize that both groups were agreed that the state had a vital role to play in the life of the church. Like their Roman Catholic opponents, most sixteenth-century Protestants could not envision a world where state and church were not working together for the cause of Christ.

Rejecting the idea of a state church
There were, however, a small number of individuals who refused to identify themselves with this way of thinking. These men and women rejected the idea of a national church to which every individual in the state belonged, along with its support in infant baptism. In other words, they rejected the idea of Christendom and repudiated what Canadian historian Ken Davis once described as "all attempts at political coercion of human conscience or a coerced Christianization of culture."

Instead, they advocated a radical alternative: churches should be composed solely of believers who were admitted on the basis of a personal confession of faith and believer's baptism. These Anabaptists ("Re-baptizers"), as they came to be called, also denounced the idea of spreading the gospel by force of arms. Rather they sought to spread it by evangelism, martyrdom, and good works.

Believer's baptism and the emergence of the Anabaptists
The key issue that marked the emergence of this radical wing of the Reformation was that of baptism. In his 1520 tract *On the Babylonian Captivity of the Church*, Martin Luther had argued that the efficacy of a sacrament was linked to the recipient's faith. He had been thinking of the Lord's Supper. But it was not long before some people applied this conviction to baptism.

In Luther's own camp at Wittenberg, one of the first to do so was Luther's "pernickety" academic colleague Andreas Bodenstein von Karlstadt around 1523. Two years later this position had been reached by a group of Swiss Anabaptists based in Zurich, where Huldreich Zwingli was active in reform, and whose key leaders were Conrad Grebel and Felix Manz.

The meaning of baptism

What did baptism mean for these early Anabaptists? Conrad Grebel put it this way in a letter he wrote to a fellow Anabaptist, Thomas Müntzer, in 1524. Baptism

> signifies that, by faith and the blood of Christ, sins have been washed away for him who is baptized ... it signifies that a man is dead and ought to be dead to sin and walks in newness of life and spirit ... the water does not confirm or increase faith ... Also baptism does not save.

When a believer is baptized as a believer, the German Anabaptist leader Balthasar Hubmaier argued in his tract *The Sum of a Christian Life* (1525), that person indicates that he or she

> has already surrendered himself according to the Word, will, and rule of Christ to live henceforth for him, to regulate all his actions according to him, to fight under his flag unto death, and to allow himself to be baptized with external water in which he publicly confesses his faith and intention.

The main concern of the early Anabaptists

For these early Anabaptists, believer's baptism was the doorway to a life of ongoing transformation as they sought to live as disciples of Christ in community with like-minded believers. Baptism thus followed from the conviction that the local church was a voluntary fellowship.

By and large these Swiss and German Anabaptists shared the conviction with Luther that "faith alone makes us righteous before God," to quote the words of Hubmaier. But the Anabaptists' main concern was elsewhere: it was on the Christian life as a life of holiness and on discipleship. They were concerned primarily with the question, "How should a

Christian live?" And answering this question shaped their distinctive witness that we shall look at in more detail next week.

24

The best of Anabaptist thought

Very few of the Anabaptists, whom we began to look at last week, were trained theologians. This meant that there was a range of theological diversity among the Anabaptists. Some denied the Trinity, some affirmed that Christ's humanity was eternal, "celestial flesh," and some rejected the Bible as the inspired Word of God. Not surprisingly, the theological errors of such people marred the entire movement for mainstream Reformers like Luther and John Calvin. But the movement really needs to be judged on the best of its thinking.

The Schleitheim Confession

A good window into the best of evangelical Anabaptist thought can be found through the *Schleithheim Confession*, drawn up in February 1527 by Swiss and South German Anabaptists at Schleitheim, a small village near the border of Germany and Switzerland. Its primary author is usually regarded as Michael Sattler, who died in 1527.

There are seven main affirmations, which deal with those areas in which the Anabaptists saw themselves differing from the Magisterial Reformers in terms of practice. As Meic Pears has noted, the *Schleitheim Confession* told its readers, "not so much what to believe, as what to do; the beliefs were implicit in the practice."

Church life

First, with regard to baptism, it was confessed: "Baptism shall be given to all those who have been taught repentance and the amendment of life and [who] believe truly that their sins are taken away through Christ." Here, the *Schleitheim Confession* emphasized that baptism is only to be administered to those who have repented and believed in Christ. This is the position that we have already noted last week that gave rise to the name of Anabaptist

Second, there was an emphasis upon church discipline, or what the confession terms "the ban." Those who fall into "error and sin" shall "be

75

warned twice privately and the third time be publicly admonished before the entire congregation, according to the command of Christ" in Matthew 18:15–18. The ban replaced the sword, which was used by Roman Catholic and Protestant alike in restraining error.

Third, when it came to the Lord's Supper—the deeply contentious issue, if you recall, between Luther and Zwingli—it was agreed that "all those who desire to break the one bread in remembrance of the broken body of Christ and all those who wish to drink of one drink in remembrance of the shed blood of Christ ... must beforehand be united in the one body of Christ, that is the congregation of God, whose head is Christ, and that by baptism." Here, the Supper is regarded as a feast of remembrance and is restricted to baptized believers.

Living in the world

The fourth affirmation had to do with separation from the world. Christians are to have nothing to do with "all popish and repopish [that is, Protestant] works and idolatry, gatherings, church attendance," as well as having nothing to do with "the diabolical weapons of violence—such as sword, armor, and the like, ... by virtue of the word of Christ: 'you shall not resist evil.'" Here, the Anabaptists distinguished themselves from both the Roman Catholic Church and the Protestants. They also affirmed their commitment to pacifism, and their refusal to use the sword to protect the Church. Conrad Grebel had similarly maintained: "True Christian believers ... neither ... use worldly sword or war, since all killing has ceased with them."

The fifth affirmation concerned the nature of true pastoral leadership, which actually did not differ much from Protestant thinking about the pastor. Sixth, church discipline was to be enacted by "only the ban" and never with physical force. Support for this affirmation is found in Jesus' response to the woman caught in adultery in John 8. Moreover, no true Christian should serve as a magistrate: it

> does not befit a Christian to be a magistrate: the rule of the government is according to the flesh, that of the Christians according to the Spirit. ... The worldly are armed with steel and iron, but Christians are armed with the armor of God, with truth, righteousness, peace,

faith, salvation, and with the Word of God.

Finally, appeal was made to Jesus' words in Matthew 5:34–35 that Christians should never take oaths, even though these are a requirement of civil society.

Separation

The main motif of these affirmations is separation, separation not only from the world of Roman Catholicism, but also separation from that of the Protestants who were seeking to reform the Church. They were in reality seeking to go back to New Testament beginnings, leapfrog as it were over fifteen hundred years of church history, and reinstitute the true Church. This was the heart of the Anabaptist programme.

It is noteworthy that when Sattler was martyred later in 1527, the Reformer Martin Bucer wrote that he had no doubts that Sattler was "a dear friend of God, although he was a leader of the Anabaptists" and that he had died as "a martyr for Christ."

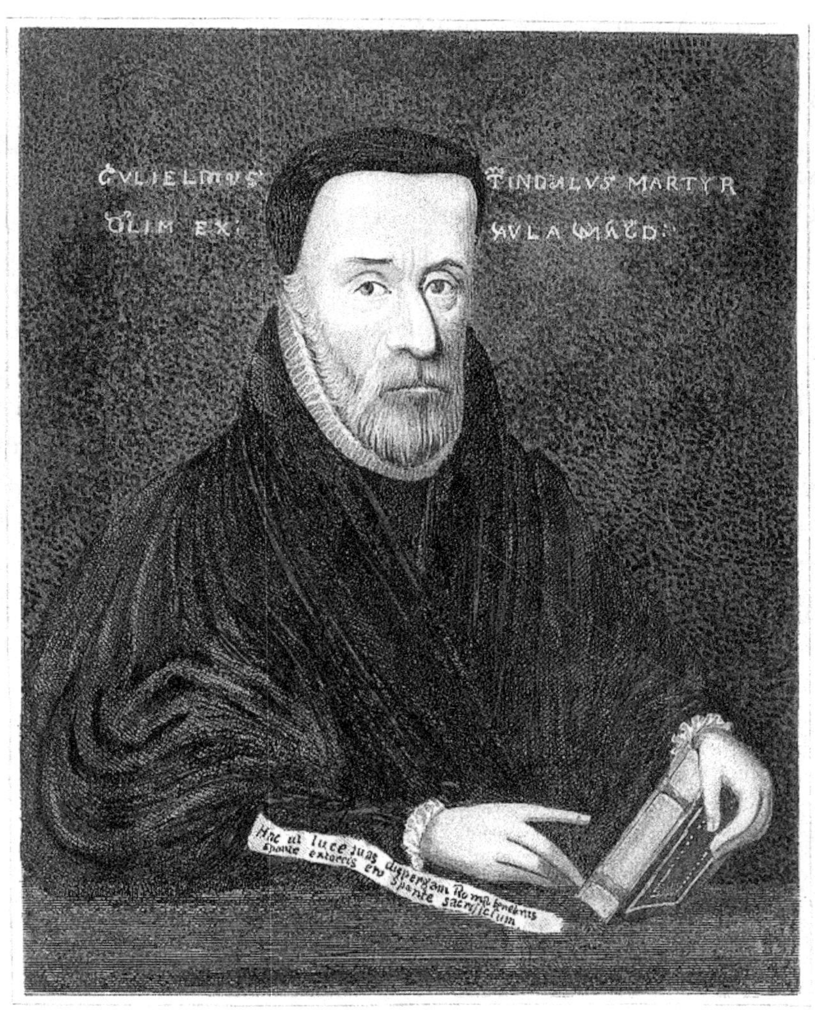

William Tyndale

25

William Tyndale's New Testament

In 1552, an English Protestant named John Rogers was on trial for his Christian faith. Rogers, who had been converted through the witness of William Tyndale, was told by Stephen Gardiner, the Lord Chancellor of Mary I and the man who was judging his case, that "thou canst prove nothing by the Scripture, the Scripture is dead: it must have a lively [i.e. living] expositor." "No," Rogers replied, "the Scriptures are alive."

Where did Rogers get such a conviction? Well, from the Bible—see, for example, Hebrews 4:12. But Rogers' conviction in this regard was also shaped by the achievement of his friend and co-worker Tyndale, whom God had used to make the Scriptures live forever in the hearts and minds of a multitude of English men and women.

Translating the New Testament

Born near Dursley in Gloucestershire, William Tyndale subsequently studied at both Oxford and Cambridge. By the early 1520s, he was a brilliant linguist, at home in the Greek of the New Testament, and eventually totally conversant with the Hebrew of the Old Testament. Convinced of the need for the English people to have the Scriptures in their own tongue (though we cannot trace in detail how he arrived at this conviction) and finding nowhere in England where he could he do such a translation, Tyndale sailed for the European continent in 1524 and eventually made his way to Martin Luther's Wittenberg.

Tyndale could have stayed in Wittenberg and translated the Scriptures in relative security and with all of the scholarly aids that he needed. Instead, he chose to go to Cologne, one of the great trading-ports of northeast Europe. It was a dangerous move since Cologne was a Roman Catholic stronghold. But Tyndale's major reason for the move undoubtedly had to have been the fact that Cologne was on the Rhine River that flowed out into the North Sea and boats would come there on trading trips from England. And Tyndale wanted his translated Scriptures to be taken to England where they could be read.

In Cologne he finished his translation of the New Testament from the Greek. All that has survived, however, is a manuscript down to Matthew 22, since, just as he was about to print it, he was betrayed to Roman Catholic authorities. Tyndale managed to escape with his translation and made his way up the Rhine to Worms.

And so it was in Worms, on the printing press of Peter Schöffer the younger (his father, Peter Schöffer the elder, had been an apprentice of the justly-famous Johann Gutenberg), that three or six thousand copies of the first printed New Testament to be translated into English out of the original Greek were run off. It was a small octavo, that is, it was made by folding each sheet three times to form a quire of eight leaves. The title-page, which is missing from two of the three copies that have survived (the recently-discovered copy in 1996 does have the title page), did not contain Tyndale's name. It reads thus: "The New Testament as it was written and caused to be written by them which heard it. To whom also our Saviour Christ Jesus commanded that they should preach it unto all creatures."

The Tyndale New Testaments were then smuggled back into England on boats, hidden in bales of cloth and other innocent-looking containers, and Tyndale's dream of giving the common person the Word of God started to become a reality. By early 1526 they were being sold openly in England.

The impact of the Tyndale New Testament
There is little doubt that Tyndale had a solid handle on the Greek language, its idioms, shades of meaning and idiosyncrasies. But equally important was his impressive grasp of the words and rhythms of the spoken English of his day. He knew how to render the Scriptures into the English vernacular so that they spoke with force and power. In fact, as Tyndale scholar David Daniell noted, "what still strikes a late-twentieth-century reader is how modern" Tyndale's translation actually is.

The reasons for this are two-fold. First, in translating the New Testament, Tyndale aimed to reproduce clear, everyday, spoken, English. And then, second, Tyndale sought to impact the heart of his readers. And John Rogers, preparing to die for the gospel of Christ in 1555, is a good example of how well Tyndale succeeded.

26

"The loss of land and life I'll reckon slight": William Tyndale's achievement

There is a portrait of William Tyndale that hangs in the dining-hall of Hertford College, Oxford. His right hand in the painting is pointing to what appears to be a Bible, under which there is a Latin couplet, of which the translation runs thus:

> To scatter Roman darkness by this light
> The loss of land and life I'll reckon slight.

This painting accurately captures Tyndale's view of God's Word—a sure and certain light in the midst of the darkness of this world—and if need be Tyndale was willing to give his life that his countrymen might have this light.

Translating the Old Testament

After completing the translation of the New Testament, which we looked at last week, Tyndale turned his attention to the Old. His translation of Genesis, which appeared in 1530, was the first English translation ever made from a Hebrew text. Only a tiny handful of Oxford and Cambridge scholars, if any at all, knew this language. In fact, most of the English population would have been astonished to discover that Hebrew had anything to do with the Bible. For them, all of their religion was wrapped up in Latin. Translations of a number of other books of the Old Testament followed: the rest of the Pentateuch in 1530 and Jonah in 1531.

Where Tyndale learned Hebrew we have no idea. It is quite unlikely he learned it in England, since so little Hebrew was known there in the 1520s. Hebrew studies only began to take root in England during the reigns of Elizabeth I and James I. He had to have learned it, therefore, on the Continent, probably in Germany. David Daniell suggests that Tyndale may have studied Hebrew at Wittenberg when he was there in the mid-1520s.

As with the Greek New Testament, Tyndale displays a wonderful facility for rendering the Hebrew Scriptures—a linguistic world utterly unlike any other in Europe at that time—into English. And coinages that he made like "Jehovah," "Passover," "scapegoat," "shewbread," and "mercy seat" have become a part of standard English.

"Permit me to have the Hebrew Bible"

By the early 1530s Tyndale was living in Antwerp, hard at work on translating Joshua to 2 Chronicles, as well as making some minor revisions to the third edition of his New Testament (1534). The translation had not yet progressed beyond the manuscript stage when he was arrested on May 21, 1535. Tyndale was betrayed into the hands of Roman Catholic authorities by a certain Henry Phillips, a perfidious individual who was probably acting under orders from John Stokesley, the Bishop of London.

He was imprisoned in the infamous prison of Vilvoorde, six miles north of Brussels. There he was put on trial for heresy—specifically for being a Lutheran—found guilty and condemned to be burned to death. Two word-pictures from the last year of his life reveal the character of the man.

The first comes from a letter that he wrote in the Vilvoorde prison in the autumn of 1535. It was found during the nineteenth century and is the only surviving example of his handwriting. Writing to the governor of the prison, Tyndale requested

> a lamp in the evening; it is indeed wearisome sitting alone in the dark. But most of all I beg and beseech your clemency to ... permit me to have the Hebrew bible, Hebrew grammar and Hebrew dictionary, that I may pass the time in that study.

Right to the very end Tyndale was intent on the study and translation of God's Word—that precious book that Tyndale knew God the Holy Spirit would use to shed the light of God's salvation throughout benighted Europe.

"Lord! open the King of England's eyes"

The other word-picture comes from the day of his death, traditionally October 6, 1536. The executioner, in an act of mercy to Tyndale, strangled him before he lit the wood piled around him. According to the martyrologist John Foxe, the last words that Tyndale was heard to utter were: "Lord! open the King of England's eyes."

Up until this point the king, Henry VIII, had been firmly opposed to the free circulation of Tyndale's translation, despite his break with Rome over his desire to get a divorce from his first wife Katherine of Aragon. Yet, within a year of Tyndale's death his New Testament was being openly published in England, though not under his name. That Tyndale was not recognized as the translator would not have bothered him at all.

27

Hugh Latimer:
England's prophet during the Reformation

Historian Iain Murray has rightly noted: "The advance of the church is ever preceded by a recovery of preaching [the Word]." The Reformation, a time of great spiritual advance, was no exception. Now, among the remarkable cadre of preachers raised up during the Reformation, the English preacher Hugh Latimer deserves more attention than he is often given in accounts of the English Reformation. The twentieth-century historian Patrick Collinson once described Latimer as one of the greatest English-speaking preachers of the sixteenth century. And according to Augustine Bernher, a Francophone pastor who was mentored by Latimer and later pastored during the reign of Elizabeth I, "if England ever had a prophet, he was one."

"The child of everlasting joy"
Hugh Latimer's father, also called Hugh Latimer, was a yeoman-farmer in Thurcaston, a small village in Leicestershire. The younger Latimer was the only son among seven siblings, and having profited from his early education, he entered Clare Hall (now Clare College) at the University of Cambridge when he was 14. He received his BA in 1510 and his MA four years later, in 1514. Around the time that he received his MA, he was ordained a priest at Lincoln. In 1524 he obtained his BD, which proved to be a key turning-point in his life.

Up until this time he had been a staunch Roman Catholic. As he stated later, "I was as obstinate a Papist as any was in England." On receiving the BD, Latimer was expected to deliver a public speech. He used the occasion to deliver a bitter attack on the teaching of Philip Melanchthon, the German Reformer and co-worker with Martin Luther. Now, among those listening to Latimer was Thomas Bilney, who was at Trinity College and the earliest of the Cambridge Reformers. Bilney was concerned by what he heard and after the lecture, he went to speak with Latimer. Latimer would later say that he learned more in the space of that conversation than he had

85

had in all of the years of his studies at Cambridge.

This then was his conversion, which can be dated to around the spring of 1524. As he stated in a sermon years later: "All the Papists think themselves to be saved by the law, and I myself was of that dangerous, perilous, and damnable opinion till I was thirty years of age." As he said on another occasion, "I am a Christian man … the child of everlasting joy, through the merits of the bitter passion of Christ."

"A weeping matter"

By the late 1520s Latimer was regularly preaching in Cambridge and in 1530 he was asked to preach before King Henry VIII. In September of 1535 Latimer's preaching gifts led to his being appointed Bishop of Worcester, which was probably the most neglected diocese in England. It had been occupied by Italian bishops for the forty years prior to Latimer becoming its bishop and not one of them had ever set foot in England. The failure of episcopal oversight in the diocese led to a lack of interest in preaching.

For instance, Latimer once came to a town where he had made arrangements beforehand to preach on the Lord's Day, and found the church locked up. He waited for half an hour for someone to show up, but no one did and when he went into the village to find out the reason why no one was at the church, he was told by one of the town's inhabitants, "Sir, this is a busy day with us, we cannot hear you; it is Robin Hood's day." Later, when recounting this incident, Latimer said that this

> is no laughing matter, my friends, it is a weeping matter, a heavy matter; a heavy matter, under the pretence of gathering for Robin Hood … to put out a preacher, to have his office less esteemed; to prefer Robin Hood before the ministration of God's Word; and all this hath come of unpreaching prelates. … If the bishops had been preachers, there should never have been any such thing.

To Latimer's way of thinking, the great calling of the bishops of England was to be preachers of the Word. Without preaching, Latimer was assured that there was no hope for England. As he rightly said: "take away preaching, and take away salvation."

28

"To suffer for God's holy Word's sake": the legacy of Hugh Latimer

The English Reformer Hugh Latimer, whose early life and conversion we looked at last week, preached hundreds of sermons, but there are only forty-one extant. Twenty-eight of these were preached at Grimsthorpe, Lincolnshire, at the estate of Katherine Willoughby, the Dowager Duchess of Suffolk, or country congregations near to her castle.

The Grimsthorpe sermons

The Grimsthorpe sermons, along with the others that are extant, were actually copied down as Latimer preached. This proved quite difficult, as the copyists struggled to keep up with what has been called "the torrent of the preacher's eloquence" and fluency. The Grimsthorpe sermons especially reveal a preacher who was able to adapt himself to his audience: he explicates a biblical text in its context, explains points of doctrine, emphasizes moral lessons, warns against the errors of the Roman Catholic Church, and all the while the sermons are suffused with passion and earnestness

Here, for example, is Latimer speaking about the necessity of knowing Christ for salvation in a sermon he preached on December 27, 1552, the day assigned to St John the Apostle in the liturgical calendar of the Western Church:

> by [Christ's] passion, which he hath suffered, he merited that as many as believe in him shall be as well justified by him, as though they themselves had never done any sin, and as though they themselves had fulfilled the law to the uttermost. For we, without him, are under the curse of the law; ... but Christ with his death hath delivered us from the curse of the law. He hath set us at liberty, and promiseth that when we believe in him, we shall not perish; the law shall not condemn us. Therefore let us study to believe in Christ. Let us put all our hope, trust, and confidence only in him; ...God hath given him unto us to be our deliverer, and to give us everlasting life. O what a joyful thing was this!

Now, during one of the Grimsthorpe sermons that Latimer preached on the petition "Thy kingdom come" from the Lord's Prayer (Matthew 6:10), he made a statement that, from the perspective of later events, can be regarded as almost predictive. "Happy is he," he said, "to whom it is given to suffer for God's holy word's sake."

Lighting a candle

Three years later, during the reign of Mary I—who was determined to destroy the evangelical faith in England and return the nation to the bosom of the Roman Church—Latimer and his fellow bishop Nicholas Ridley were called to indeed suffer death for the sake of their commitment to God's Word and its authority over all of life. Latimer had been committed to the Tower of London in September 1553, and then, in April 1554, he was taken with Ridley to the Bocardo prison in Oxford where they underwent examination of their theological beliefs.

Both were found guilty of heresy and condemned to death. While in the Bocardo, Latimer wrote the following in a lengthy letter dated May 15, 1555:

> Because you be God's sheep, prepare yourselves to the slaughter, always knowing, that in the sight of God our death is precious. ...
>
> Die once we must; how and where, we know not. Happy are they whom God giveth to pay nature's debt (I mean to die) for his sake. Here is not our home; let us therefore accordingly... [have] always before our eyes that heavenly Jerusalem, and the way thereto in persecution.

On October 16, 1555, Latimer and Ridley were taken out of Oxford through the Bocardo Gate where they were tied to a stake in what is now Broad Street. Wood was piled around the two bishops, but the wood piled around Ridley was freshly cut and thus only smoldered. Ridley was in conscious agony till the very end and at one point was heard to pray: "I cannot burn! Lord have mercy upon me!" Latimer, though, died fairly swiftly, but before he did so he uttered the following words in response to this cry by Ridley. These words, recorded by the English martyrologist John Foxe, form a fitting conclusion to any study of Latimer as a preacher, for in a sense they have a sermonic quality: "Be of good comfort Master Ridley, and play the man! We shall this day light such a candle by God's grace in England, as I trust shall never be put out."

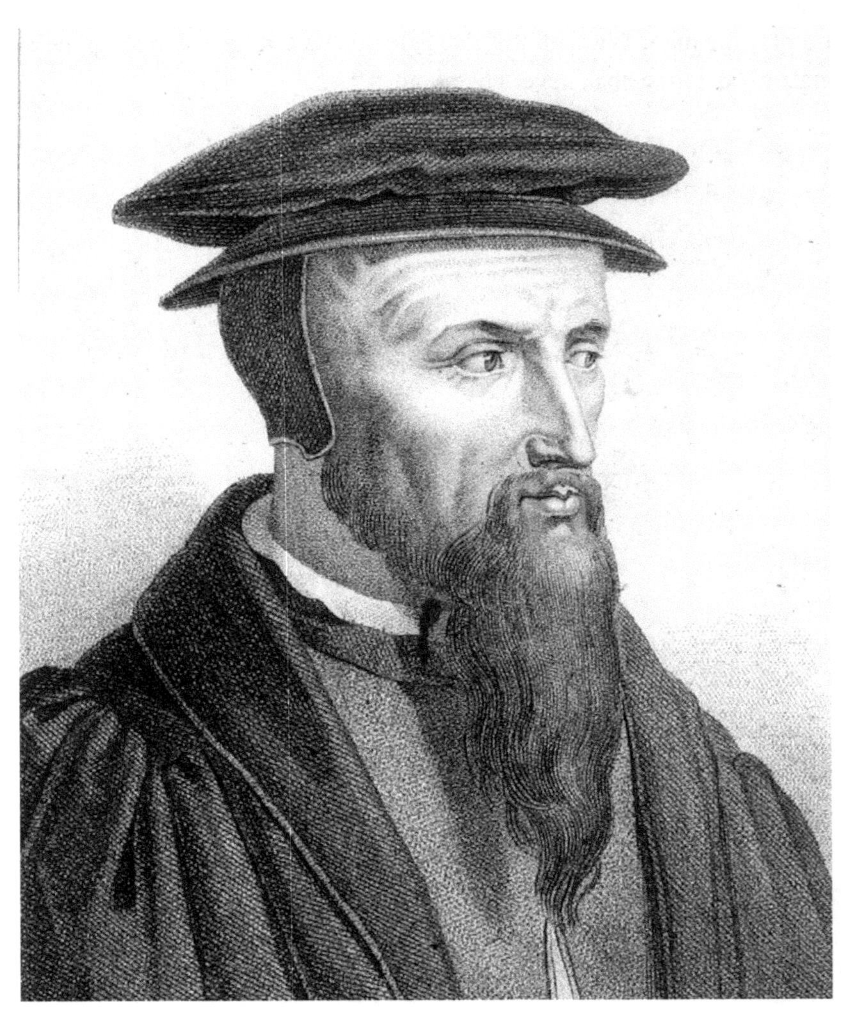

John Calvin

29
John Calvin and his *Institutes*

Between 1550 and his death in 1564, the French Reformer John Calvin's output of published words was never less than a 100,000 per year. And supreme among all of these published words were those of his *Institutes of the Christian Religion*, which once led the German Lutheran Philip Melanchthon to dub Calvin "the theologian."

Editions of Calvin's Institutes

The first edition of the *Institutes* had been published in Basle in 1536. Three years later Calvin brought out a second edition, printed in Strasbourg, that was three times as large as the first. Further editions appeared in 1543 and 1550, and then finally the fifth edition was issued in 1559 in Geneva. It is almost five times larger than the first edition.

Calvin also translated the 1539 Latin edition of the *Institutes* into French in 1541, and supervised the translation of three later French translations, the last one appearing in 1560. The French translations of Calvin's *Institutes* helped to shape the French language for generations, not unlike the influence of the King James Version on the English language.

It is noteworthy that the year after the first French edition, the French government formally banned the book in the summer of 1542 and ordered all book sellers to surrender their copies within three days. In 1559, after the final edition of the *Institutes*, Pope Paul IV placed the work on the papal *Index* of condemned works—it remained there till the *Index* was discarded in 1966.

The final Latin edition of the *Institutes* is approximately five times the length of the first edition. This significant growth of this key work betrays an essential characteristic of Calvin the theologian: teachability. But it would be a mistake to suppose that one can grasp the totality of Calvin's theology by simply absorbing the 1559 edition of the *Institutes*. His commentaries, sermons, treatises, catechisms, and correspondence reveal other aspects and nuances of his theology that must be taken into account in any reflection on his theology as a whole.

The title of the Institutes

The English translation of the title of Calvin's work is *The Institutes of the Christian Religion* or simply Calvin's *Institutes*. This title, however, may not be the best translation from the original Latin, *Institutio Christianae Religionis*.

The Latin word *religio* in Calvin's day did not have its modern definition as "religion." The word *religio* comes from the Latin verb *religare*, "to bind," and used in a theological sense would be a reference to the bond that unites humans to God, as exemplified in the late medieval period by the monastic vow. The phrase *Christianae religionis* then would indicate the "Christian bond" to God or what came to be called Christian piety or even the Christian life.

The Latin word *institutio* can mean "arrangement, custom, introduction, or education." A more accurate English title might then be *An Introduction to Christian Piety*. But the current English title is quite well established and unlikely to be replaced.

The purpose of the Institutes

This reflection on the meaning of the title is important to understand what Calvin is doing in the book. He is not presenting a merely intellectual discussion of the doctrines of true Christianity. He is not even beginning with a first principle like the sovereignty of God and building a theological edifice upon this founding principle. Rather, as one author, Jean-Daniel Benoit, has put it: "the *Institutes* is ... a book of piety more than a dogmatic treatise."

And yet, the work is not simply a discussion of Christian spirituality. Rather, it describes how a person, brought face to face with the living God in the Scriptures, is to think about this God and himself/herself. It is experiential theology at its very best.

30

"The sweetest harmony":
John Calvin's reflections on marriage

Compared to the marriages of other famous Reformers, we know comparatively little about John Calvin's marriage to Idelette van Buren (aka Idelette de Bure). For example, Martin Luther's famous marriage to Katharina von Bora, which we considered a few weeks ago, became something of a public exemplar for Protestants. Not so Calvin's marriage, which was very much in line with Calvin's habitual reticence to go public about his personal affairs. Yet, in the year following Idelette's death in 1549, he stated in his little tract *Concerning Scandals* (1550) that Idelette was "a rare woman."

Marriage to Idelette

Idelette van Buren's roots were originally in the Netherlands and she may well have come from the town of Buren in the province of Gelderland. Be this as it may, her first husband Jean Stordeur was a Walloon from Liège, today in Belgium. For a time Jean and his wife Idelette were convinced Anabaptists. And it was as a prominent Anabaptist that Jean had first met Calvin in Geneva in March 1537 when Jean came to the city for a discussion between the Anabaptists and the Reformed pastors. Two years later, now in Strasbourg, Calvin had succeeded in convincing Jean and Idelette to embrace Reformed theology, and they became members of the French congregation that Calvin was pastoring in Strasbourg.

It was not long after this that Jean died of the plague in the spring of 1540. Calvin had obviously gotten to know Idelette initially through the discussions she and her husband had had with Calvin about the Reformed faith. Then, when Jean was dying Calvin would have seen more of Idelette when he made pastoral visits to their home. What he saw of her made such a deep impression on him that by August 17, 1540, Calvin had married her. Although Calvin often emphasized that external beauty was not to be a key determinant in marriage, Idelette was, according to Farel, very pretty.

Intimate allies

Now, we get a fabulous insight into Idelette's character in a letter that Calvin wrote after her death on March 29, 1549. It was addressed to his close friend Pierre Viret and written on April 7, 1549. In it Calvin stated:

> Although the death of my wife has been exceedingly painful to me, yet I subdue my grief as well as I can. …you know well enough how tender, or rather soft, my mind is. Had not a powerful self-control, therefore, been vouchsafed to me, I could not have borne up so long. And truly mine is no common source of grief. I have been bereaved of the best possible companion of my life, of one, who, had it been so ordered, would not only have been the willing sharer of my indigence, but even of my death. During her life she was my faithful co-labourer in my ministry.

Here, in the space of a few lines from his sorrowing heart, Calvin sums up the Reformed understanding of marriage: it is a union of intimate allies. Idelette had been the "best possible companion" of his life, one who had been a "faithful co-labourer" in his ministry.

Marriage defined by Genesis 2

Behind Calvin's understanding of marriage lies Genesis 2:18–24, where we are told that Adam's being alone is not "good," which is striking in view of the fact that everything else that God had made to that point is said to have been good. So, we read in this passage, that God made Adam a "helper," a word, according to Calvin's commentary on this text, which goes to the heart of his understanding of marriage. As the French Reformer comments on this passage in Genesis:

> Now, since God assigns the woman as a help to the man, he … pronounces that marriage will really prove to men the best support of life. …The vulgar proverb, indeed, is, that she is a necessary evil; but the voice of God is rather to be heard, which declares that woman is given as a companion and an associate to the man, to assist him to live well.

But the fallenness of humanity—which, in Calvin's day, had issued in the unbiblical perspectives on marriage, celibacy, and sexuality promoted by Roman Catholic theologians—has deeply disfigured God's intentions for the holy estate of marriage. As Calvin went on to delineate: "if the integrity of man had remained to this day such as it was from the beginning, ... the sweetest harmony would reign in marriage."

And it was this conviction about marriage, rooted as it was in solid reflection on Scripture, that led Calvin to make such wide-ranging statements about marriage as that it is "the sacred bond," "a holy fellowship," "a divine partnership," "a loving association," "the best support of life," and "the holiest kind of company in all the world."

31

Calvin and the Servetus affair:
learning from the faults of a Reformer

"The past is a foreign country; they do things differently there." This famous first line by Leslie Poles Hartley in his novel *The Go-Between* (1953) has long been a favourite maxim that orients my teaching of history, for it is notoriously difficult to treat former eras of history with any degree of empathy that they need to make them understandable. A classic example is afforded by what has been called the Servetus Affair in Geneva in 1553, when John Calvin was embroiled in the trial and execution by burning of Michael Servetus, who was adamant in his denial of the Trinity. Calvin's involvement in this gruesome incident has given rise to his posthumous reputation as a bloody tyrant who ran Geneva like some sort of gulag.

Calvin and heresy

Calvin could certainly be vicious in his verbal attacks on those whom he regarded as heretics and his theological opponents, but there is *no evidence* that he regularly sought to kill them. Thus, theologians who crossed swords with Calvin in Geneva—men like Jérôme-Hermès Bolsec and Sebastian Castellio—were exiled from the city. Moreover, is vital to note that most sixteenth-century Christian figures, both Protestant and Roman Catholic, regarded heresy not simply as a wrong-headed intellectual pathway, but as imbued with the stain of moral filth, and as such it had to be cut out of the body politic lest it pollute the entire community. If the Genevan authorities had let Servetus live once he had been recognized and arrested in the city, it would have given the enemies of the Reformation, notably the Roman Catholic Church, proof that the Reformers were also heretics for tolerating such heresy.

Moreover, Calvin's political standing in Geneva was still tenuous in the early 1550s. Many of the city's patricians looked askance at the French Reformer and would have been all too happy to boot him out as they had once done in 1538. In fact, one of Calvin's co-Reformers, Wolfgang Musculus, was convinced that Servetus had come to Geneva on purpose to exploit the differences between Calvin and the city council. Although Calvin's deep dislike of Servetus was all too clear during the 1550s, he simply did not have the power to execute the heretic. The charge by the nineteenth-century J.B. Galiffé that Calvin was a "tyrant priest who submitted Geneva to the most infamous servitude" is patently wrong, failing as it does to understand the severe limitations on Calvin's political power.

There were indeed others who were put to death during Calvin's ministry in Geneva. During an outbreak of the plague in Geneva during 1544–1545, some thirty-eight men and women were accused of aiding its spread and subsequently executed for what we would call bio-terrorism today. Calvin appears to have believed this charge about these sixteenth-century bio-terrorists, who were accused of smearing plague-contaminated ointment on the key-holes of Genevan houses! One other execution was that of Jacques Gruet in 1547, a materialist who may also have been an atheist. He was executed not for his beliefs, though, but for threatening the life of Calvin and seeking to instigate a coup in the city. Not surprisingly the numbers of those executed in Geneva during Calvin's time were exaggerated by his enemies, exaggerations that were bandied about especially in the eighteenth and nineteenth centuries when Calvinism (a word that Calvin loathed) was often a house under attack.

Learning from Calvin

Now, this not to whitewash Calvin. In his own day, Castellio rightly remonstrated with Calvin for executing Servetus. The state has no biblical mandate, under the new covenant, to execute heretics. Rather, what Calvin actually did and did not do needs to be set forth as well understanding those actions in the context of his times. Moreover, it goes without saying, in the opinion of this author, that the truly blameworthy aspects of Calvin's life noted above do not lessen some of the vital truths that can be learned from his life and witness.

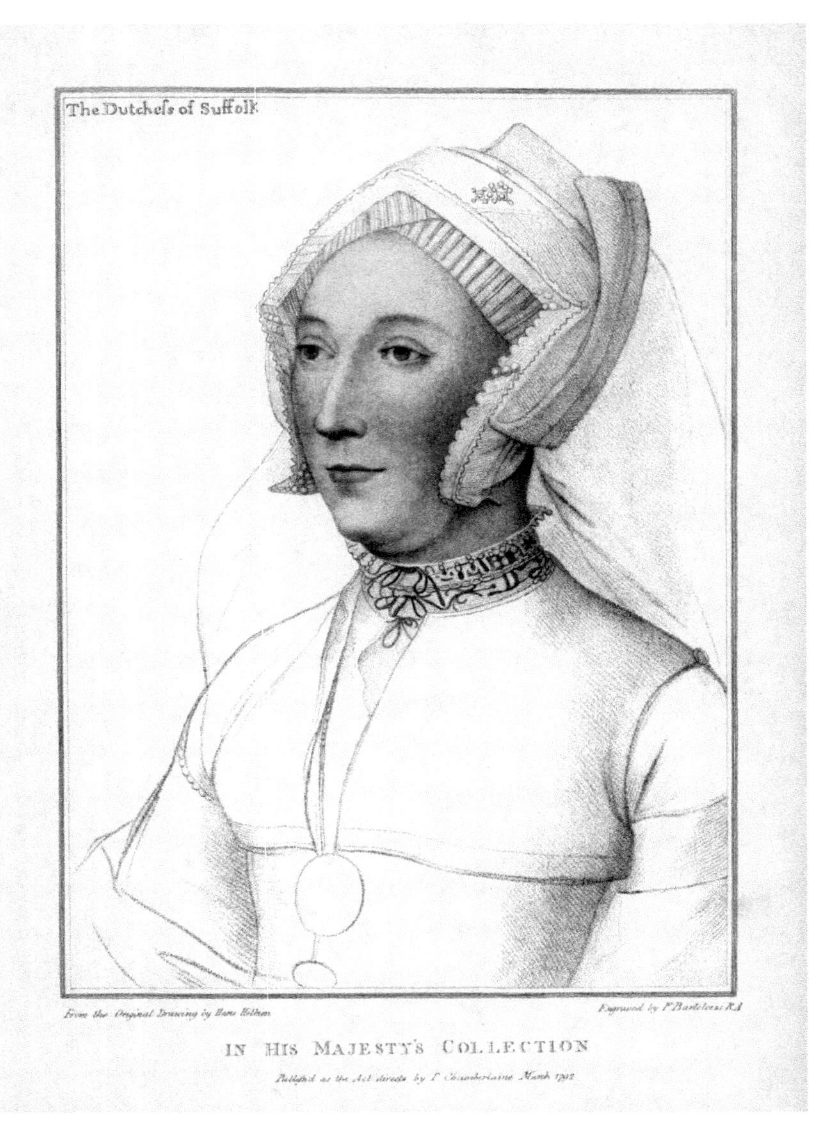

Katherine Willoughby, the Duchess of Suffolk

32

Katherine Willoughby, the Puritan Duchess

Recently, British historian Alec Ryrie has described Katherine Willoughby as an "evangelical firebrand" and perhaps "the most aggressive of the reformers" within the royal circle around Henry VIII. In her own day, a hostile Spanish Roman Catholic source described her as "one of the worst heretics in England."

Early years and marriage to Charles Brandon
Katherine Willoughby's life began in a staunch Roman Catholic environment. Her mother was an ardent Spanish Roman Catholic by the name of Doña Maria Sarmiento de Salinas, who was the confidante and favourite lady–in-waiting of Queen Katherine of Aragon, the first wife of Henry VIII. Maria probably named her only daughter after the Queen.

Her first marriage was to Charles Brandon, the first Duke of Suffolk and a close friend of Henry VIII: she was only fourteen and he was 49! Throughout the 1530s, despite the massive religious changes that were taking place in England, Katherine Willoughby, now Katherine Brandon and the Duchess of Suffolk, remained a committed Roman Catholic.

Katherine Willoughby's Evangelicalism
When was Katherine Brandon converted to evangelical convictions? It was probably during her time as a lady-in-waiting within the household of the evangelical Queen, Katherine Parr, Henry VIII's sixth and final wife. By the mid-1540s, Katherine believed that Scripture was the supreme guide to the Christian Faith. She had acquired a copy of William Tyndale's New Testament and begun to be openly critical of Roman Catholicism.

After her husband Charles Brandon died in August of 1545, Katherine became more open in her commitment to evangelical views. By the late 1540s she had rejected the concept of transubstantiation and that we can be saved by faith and works. And in the late 1550s she came to embrace the doctrines of predestination and election.

As one of the wealthiest women in England she began to use her wealth to support the cause of reform. In Lincolnshire, for example, she did all she could to ensure that every parish church had a copy of the Bible. When the great German reformer Martin Bucer came to Cambridge as Regius Professor of Divinity in 1549, Katherine befriended him. She also served as the patron of various leading evangelical preachers and reformers, of whom the chief was Hugh Latimer, the great Tudor preacher who had the greatest influence on Katherine's faith and seems to have been something of a spiritual mentor to Katherine.

Marriage to Richard Bertie and exile

By 1552 the Duchess was firmly in love with a man named Richard Bertie. Although he was not a nobleman, they were married by Hugh Latimer in either 1552 or 1553.

With the accession of the fanatical Roman Catholic Mary I to the throne in 1553, however, Katherine and her new husband were in danger of being incarcerated or being subjected to religious demands that would violate their conscience. It became clear to Katherine and Richard that they needed to quit England and flee to the European continent. It is noteworthy that Katherine was prepared to relinquish all of her lands and wealth, aristocratic standing and position, for the sake of her evangelical faith. They eventually found a place of refuge in Poland.

Evidence of Katherine's faith

Mary I died in 1558 and it was now safe to return to England. As soon as Katherine heard that Elizabeth I had become queen she wrote the following letter to the new queen. The text is a key window into her evangelical faith.

> The almighty and ever-living God so endue your Majesty with his Spirit, that it may be said of you, as of his prophet David, "He hath found one even after his own heart." … now is our season, if ever anywhere, of rejoicing, and to say, after Zachary, "Blessed be the Lord God of Israel", which hath visited and delivered your Majesty, and by you us, His and your miserable and afflicted subjects. For if the Israelites might joy in their Deborah, how much we English in our Elizabeth that deliverance of our thralled conscience. … I

greedily wait and pray to the Almighty to … give me a prosperous journey once again presently to see your Majesty, to rejoice together with my countryfolks, and to sing a song to the Lord in my native land.

The return to England and frustration

Katherine and Richard travelled back to England in the late spring or summer of 1559. Like many of those who came to be called Puritans, however, she was ultimately disappointed by the Queen's religious policy. While Elizabeth shared many of the Puritans' theological convictions, she insisted that she was the head of the church and was tolerant of worship practices in the church that reminded the Puritans of medieval Catholicism. As Katherine noted in a letter to William Cecil, the Queen's first minister, "Christ … hath left his Gospel behind him a rule sufficient and only to be followed."

In the final twenty years of her life, Katherine was disappointed with the Elizabethan settlement. Well has Paul Zahl described her as "a frustrated Puritan" during this period of her life and spoken of her "insistent impatience with Elizabeth" and her "snail's pace in the Reformation of the Church." This impatience began with the issue of reforming the Church, but overflowed into more personal matters. She long petitioned Elizabeth to give her husband the title of Duke, but all to no avail. A number of her final letters relate to this worldly matter and Katherine's frustration that Elizabeth would not listen to her.

When Katherine died in 1580 her husband Richard had a sculptor by the name of Thomas Goodlord erect a huge memorial to his wife in the parish church of St. James, Spilsby, which also became a memorial to him as well, when he died two years later. On the back of the memorial, which is quite visible to anyone in the sanctuary, are six panels of texts, five in Latin and one in English. One of them, in Latin, expresses Katherine and Richard's hope: "We know that our Redeemer lives, and we believe that we shall rise again out of the dust and though after our skin worms destroy our bodies, yet shall we see God in our flesh, and not another."

33

Richard Greenham:
architect of Puritan pastoral piety

For much of the seventeenth century, Richard Greenham was reckoned to be among the three or four most important figures of the Elizabethan Church of the late sixteenth century, being especially renowned for his skill as a spiritual guide. In fact, T.D. Bozeman has remarked that Greenham needs to be regarded as "the foremost architect of the first great awakening of [English] Protestant piety." And yet, as his recent biographer Eric Josef Carlson has noted, "for centuries he has almost vanished from the historical record, thanks to his decision to labor in the relatively obscure rural Cambridgeshire parish of Dry Drayton," a few miles to the north of Cambridge.

Prior to Greenham's 1559 matriculation at Pembroke Hall in Cambridge University, we have no accurate knowledge of his birthplace and early years. After nearly a dozen years of study at Cambridge, Greenham spent the bulk of his pastoral career, from 1570 to 1590, in the small parish of St. Peter and St. Paul, Dry Drayton, then a community of about 150 people. Greenham moved to London in 1590 for reasons now unknown. Of his ministry there we know next to nothing, but it seems he came to regret this move. He died in April 1594 of unknown causes.

The Puritan preacher of Dry Drayton
In a letter to the bishop of Ely, Greenham described his ministry as "preaching Christ crucified unto myself and country people." Greenham summed up his pastoral ministry as "none other thing, but to preach the word of God sincerely, and purely with a care of the glory of God and a desire of the salvation of our brethren." And again, Greenham could state: "such horrible disorder is there, where God's Word is not truly preached." And again, he could argue, "there is no other means in the world to come unto Christ than by the preaching of the word."

Deeply concerned to educate his hearers—female illiteracy in the parish was virtually one hundred percent, while male illiteracy was about seventy percent—and due to the fact that numerous demands on his time gave him little free time, Greenham would rise at four every day to study and prepare his sermons. During the week he preached a sermon on Monday, Tuesday, Wednesday, and Friday just after dawn so that his parishioners might attend before they went to work. After preaching he went back to study in the morning, and then in the afternoon he visited the sick or went out into the fields to speak with his parishioners who were working there. He also preached twice on Sundays, and on Thursday morning he catechized the children of the parish, which he also did each Sunday evening.

According to Henry Holland, a London pastor who prepared a posthumous edition of Greenham's works and wrote a short memoir of the Puritan pastor to accompany this edition, Greenham preached with such energy that "his shirt would usually be as wet with sweating as if it had been drenched in water." Before he went into the pulpit, though, he often experienced what he came to believe were Satanic attacks, being assailed by "very sharp and trembling fears in the flesh."

A counseling ministry

Though well known and appreciated as a gospel preacher, it was as a pastoral counselor that Greenham excelled. According to Holland, the fame of Greenham's skill as a spiritual counselor spread far and wide so that many, who "groaned under spiritual afflictions and temptations," came to see him and "by his knowledge and experience many were restored to joy and comfort." Thomas Fuller (1608–1661), whose father knew Greenham, similarly said that "his masterpiece was in comforting wounded consciences ... God used him herein as an instrument of good to many, who came to him with weeping eyes and went from him with cheerful souls."

Greenham's friends came to regard Greenham as "the paradigmatic godly pastor" and hoped he would write a book on the art of spiritual nurture, but he never did. A series of his choice sayings was drawn up, however, after his death. The following examples of these sayings below do indeed reveal Greenham to be a man of true wisdom—the final one is indeed noteworthy for it reveals Greenham's deep love for the souls of his people:

- "Many are barren in grace because they are barren in prayer."
- "Where the Scripture hath not a mouth, we ought not to have ears."
- "There is nothing so precious, as God's grace, which changeth the face of heaven and earth; and nothing so vile as sin, who openeth hell, and staineth the earth, and shutteth up heaven."
- "It would be a thousand deaths, yea, a thousand hells unto me, to see your souls miscarry."

Mentoring pastors

Yet, for all his godliness, insight, evangelical message and hard work, his ministry initially appeared to be virtually fruitless. Others outside his parish were apparently blessed through it, but not, it seems, his own people. A little rhyme that expressed this fact made the rounds among the Puritans: "Greenham had pastures green, but flocks full lean." And as he himself said to Richard Warfield, who succeeded him as parish minister: "I perceive no good wrought by my ministry on any but one family."

But like many other ministers of the gospel, Greenham was not a good judge of the real impact of his ministry. In the rural England of Greenham's day, there was much fallow ground to be broken up. It was a time for sowing; the time for reaping still lay in the future. And through Greenham's influence on a number of key Puritan ministers of the next generation, men like Arthur Hildersham, Henry Smith, and Richard Rogers whom he personally mentored, it came to pass that thousands of English men and women were, by the 1620s, in some sense the spiritual flock of Richard Greenham.

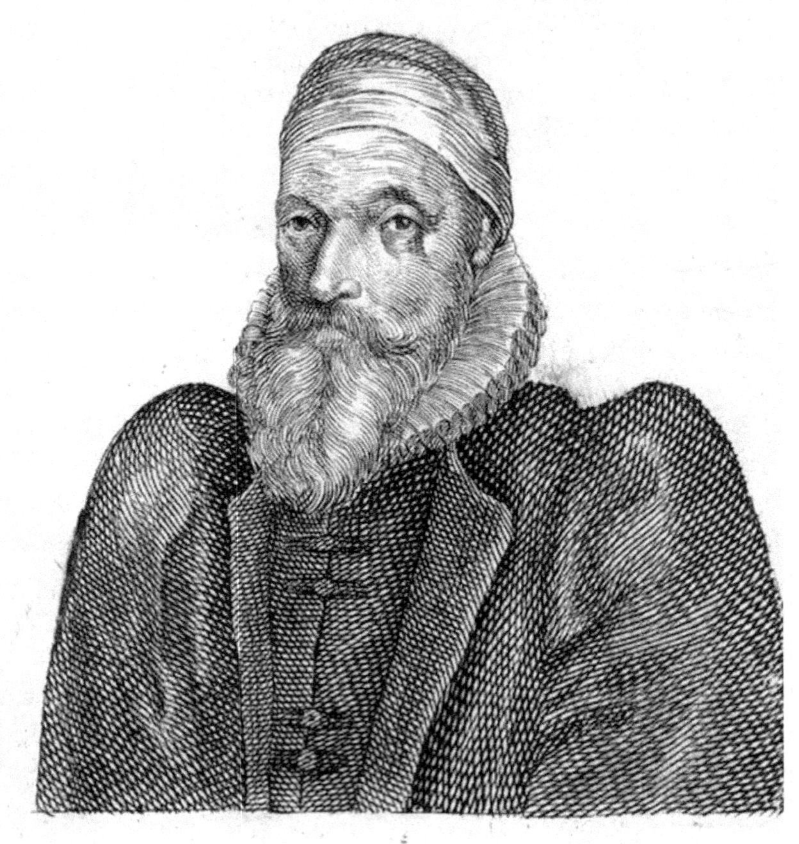

John Rogers

34

Roaring John Rogers

When John Rogers first went up to Emmanuel College, Cambridge, as a student in February 1588, he proved to be a complete wastrel. His way was being paid by his uncle, a well-known Puritan preacher by the name of Richard Rogers, but John sold all of his books so as to spend the proceeds on various sinful pastimes. Not surprisingly, John was asked to leave Emmanuel College, a hotbed of Puritan theology and piety. Richard Rogers' wife Barbara, though, convinced her husband to intervene with college authorities and give the young man another opportunity. So, the younger Rogers went up again to Cambridge, only to prove the profligate once more, again selling his books and squandering the money obtained on his vices. His uncle was about to wash his hands of him at that point, but yielding once again to the entreaties of Barbara, John was sent up to Cambridge yet a third time. This time things proved to be quite different as a long-suffering God saved the young man, and Richard later confessed, "I will never despair of a man for John Rogers' sake."

At Dedham

Most of Rogers' pastoral ministry after graduation was spent at what was then a Puritan stronghold in the parish of Dedham, Essex. He came to St. Mary the Virgin in Dedham in 1605 and served there as a lecturer till his death thirty-one years later. A good number of Puritan leaders who had conscientious objections about aspects of the liturgy of the Church of England served as lecturers since this enabled them to preach, usually on a Sunday afternoon, outside of the framework of the typical Anglican service. Rogers was said to be an extraordinary preacher, both a "Boanerges, a Son of Thunder" (see Mark 3:17)—hence his nickname, "Roaring John Rogers"—and "a Barnabas, a Son of Consolation" (see Acts 4:36), through whose preaching many were led in submission to Christ.

A remarkable outpouring of the Spirit

The great Puritan theologian Thomas Goodwin was present on one occasion when, during the course of a sermon, Rogers took the part of God, angry with his people for not prizing the Scriptures and not reading them. He threatened to take away the Bible from such an ungrateful people. Rogers then impersonated the people, falling to his knees in the pulpit, and pleading with God not to give them a famine of hearing the Word of God. "Lord, whatsoever thou dost to us, take not thy Bible from us; kill our children, burn our houses, destroy our goods, only spare us thy Bible, take not away thy Bible."

Goodwin recalled that the impact of the sermon was electrifying, as many of the people in the church were smitten in their consciences and reduced to copious weeping in repentance. Goodwin himself, not yet converted, was brought under deep conviction of sin. When he came out of the church he was so overwhelmed with tears that he stood for fifteen minutes or so, leaning on the neck of his horse before he had the strength to mount. The Puritans long prayed and laboured for a national awakening, and though these prayers and labours did not see an answer in their lifetime—such an awakening was to come in the eighteenth century—here we clearly see an anticipation, an antepast, of the remarkable scenes of revival in the next century. Here is great encouragement not to give up praying if we do not see immediate fruit. Praying breath is never lost.

Love for the lost

Among Rogers' few publications was *A Treatise of Love*, which had begun life as a series of sermons on 1 John 3:3. It is often said that the Puritans had little vision for evangelism beyond their own world, but a quick perusal of this work soon raises questions about the truth of this supposed "fact." One of the marks of true love for God, Rogers asserts, is that it longs that others love God as well and so seeks "to draw as many to God" as it can.

In fact, Christian love has a global reach, for it "reacheth to all, near and far, strangers, enemies, within and without the pale of the Church, Turks [that is, Muslims] and pagans, we must pray for them, & do them any good if they come in our way." In fact, Rogers explicitly argues that "we must pray for the poor pagans, that God would send his light and truth among them, that they in time may be brought into the bosom of the Church, and the sheepfold of Christ Jesus." God also answered these prayers—but again in his time, when, in the late eighteenth century, we see the advent of the modern missionary movement.

35

The church and the bubonic plague
in later Stuart England

As we saw a few weeks ago, the church has not always responded to epidemics or pandemics well. But one sterling occasion when she did, was during the outbreak of the bubonic plague in southern England in 1665.

The impact of the plague

There were outbreaks of the bubonic plague in England a number of times during the seventeenth century: in 1603, 1625, 1636 and 1665, with at least 30,000 dying of the plague in London alone in 1603, and 35,000 in 1625, 10,000 in 1636 and 68,596 recorded deaths in 1665. By 1665 the city population of London had reached almost half a million and this means at least one-seventh died of the plague in 1665. The eminent Puritan author Richard Baxter reckoned in his autobiography that the number of dead was closer to a hundred thousand people, which would be about a fifth of London's population. Richard Baxter noted, "It is scarce possible for people that live in a time of health and security, to apprehend the dreadfulness of that pestilence! ... O how sinfully unthankful are we for our quiet societies, habitations and health!"

Baxter also noted that: "The richer sort removing out of the City, the greatest blow fell on the poor." This would be one negative effect that persisted into the eighteenth century when even though the plague was no longer present, thinking about the plague was still having a big effect on the English psychologically. And it was the poor who were regarded as the potential source of another outbreak: their very bodies were regarded as being prone to generating and spreading contagious disease.

Preaching the gospel

Baxter noted that "one great benefit the plague brought to the city" was that Nonconformist ministers who had been forbidden to preach since 1662 (due to the repressive government of Charles II), stayed in the city when most of the Anglican ministers fled the capital. Though forbidden to preach, these Nonconformist ministers began to proclaim the gospel to all who would listen—and the churches were crowded. Before this they had been preaching in rented rooms—"secret narrow meetings," Baxter calls them. But the plague, Baxter went on, "brought them ... into public."

Precious words of James Janeway

Among the ministers whom Baxter mentions was active in preaching during this time was a young man by the name of James Janeway, whose sermons during this period were published after the plague as *Heaven Upon Earth; or The best Friend in the Worst Times* (1667). Among his emphases in these sermons was that men and women need to find succour in God as the friend of his people. In his words:

> Another glorious effect of acquaintance with God, is, that it makes a man like God, which is the top of the creature's honour. Company is of an assimilating nature. He that before was unholy, and like the Devil; by conversion to God, and converse with him is made holy like God. ... O how doth such a one shine! What a majesty, glory, and beauty is there in his face! ... A full and perfect conformity and likeness to God is the very glory of glory ... O why stand you then so far off from God! Come nearer him, and the rays of his glorious Image will reflect from your lives; Be acquainted with him, and you shall be like him; keep much in his company by faith, secret prayer, and meditation, and you will be more holy, divine, spiritual.

And this is still precious, and sweet advice in our trying times!

36

Margaret Charlton Baxter:
a Puritan wife

If I were asked by anyone to recommend one solid book on marriage, I would turn to the Puritans—not the prudes modern Western culture think they were—and recommend the appropriate sections dealing with the married estate in *The Christian Directory* by Richard Baxter of Kidderminster. According to J.I. Packer, Baxter, along with other Puritan authors, gave marriage "such strength, substance, and solidity as to warrant the verdict that…under God…they were creators of the English Christian marriage." In Baxter's case, his rich understanding of marriage was indebted both to his knowledge of the Word of God on this subject and to his own marriage to Margaret Charlton.

Margaret had been converted under Baxter's preaching at Kidderminster. Like Baxter, she came from Shropshire—she had, in fact, been raised only a few miles from where Baxter grew up, though in considerably wealthier circumstances. Initially, when Margaret heard Baxter's preaching, she had little liking for either him or the people of the town. She had, Baxter tells us in his life of Margaret—*A Breviate of the Life of Margaret…Charlton*—a "great aversion to the poverty and strictness of the people" of the town. Frivolous and held by the gaieties of this world, she was far more interested in "glittering herself in costly apparel." The Holy Spirit, though, was at work in her life. A series of sermons that Baxter preached on the doctrine of conversion was, Baxter tells us, "received on her heart as the seal on the wax." Her spiritual transformation was swift and genuine. One of the first signs of this radical change in her life was "her fervent, secret prayers."

Ministry in London

Richard and Margaret were married in 1662, only two weeks after Baxter and some two thousand other Puritan ministers were excluded from their pulpits by the state for refusing to agree to worship according to the letter of *The Book of Common Prayer*. Known as a key leader among the Puritans, Richard was dogged by spies until toleration in 1688. He was the frequent object of slander,

115

and on one occasion arrested and imprisoned. He and Margaret went to live in London, where they were forced to move house frequently and often lived in what could only be called wretched circumstances. One gets a good idea of the nature of Margaret's mettle when Baxter tells us that at the time of his imprisonment in 1669, Margaret "cheerfully went with me into prison."

Despite the fact that it was illegal for Baxter to preach, Margaret more than once used large portions of her wealth to pay for chapels to be built for her husband's ministry. On one occasion in 1673, she asked him where in London he most desired to preach. He told her, "St. Martin's Parish, where are said to be forty thousand more than can come into the Church, … where … many live like Americans [that is, the Indigenous Peoples], and have heard no sermon of many years." So Margaret set out to have a chapel built in this parish on a vacant lot.

Baxter preached the first Sunday after its completion, but was absent the following week since he had to preach at another locale outside of London. A Mr. Seddon agreed to take place Baxter's place. State officials, though, had learned about the venture and were determined to arrest Baxter for illegal preaching. Getting a warrant for his arrest they descended on the chapel. Not finding Baxter, though, they arrested Seddon in his stead and put him in prison for a number of months. Margaret felt Seddon's imprisonment keenly and blamed herself. She used her own funds to visit and comfort him in the prison, pay all of his lawyer's fees, and also support his family.

There were some who blamed Margaret for busying "her head so much about churches, and works of charity" and not being "content to live privately and quietly." But Baxter defended her: "this is but just what profane unbelievers say against all zeal and spiritual godliness … Doth not Paul call some women his helps in the gospel?"—a reference to passages like Philippians 4:3 and Romans 16:2–6.

Imperfect characters

Like every married couple, Richard and Margaret were imperfect characters. As Richard said: "My dear wife did look for more good in me than she found … We are all like pictures that must not be looked at too near. They that come near us find more faults and badness in us than others at a distance know." Yet, they managed to have a wonderful marriage. What was their secret?

Well, first, Richard and Margaret followed the advice that Richard gave to married couples in his *Christian Directory* to delight in one another:

> When husband and wife take pleasure in each other, it uniteth them in duty, it helpeth them with ease to do their work, and bear their burdens … "Rejoice with the wife of thy youth, as the loving hind and pleasant roe, let her breast satisfy thee at all times, and be thou ravished always with her love" [Proverbs 5:18–19].

Then, they had a tremendous agreement about what ultimately mattered in life: "Nothing causeth so near and fast and comfortable an union as to be united in one God, one Christ, one Spirit, one Church, one hope of heavenly glory."

37

The "coffee-man in Southwark": James Jones

The frequenting of cafés and coffee shops by many modern-day students to study, converse, and plug into the internet is actually tapping into a much older phenomenon that goes back to the late seventeenth-century and early eighteenth-century coffeehouses of England. Unlike taverns, coffeehouses came to be recognized, as historian Brian Cowan has noted in his excellent study *The Social Life of Coffee: The Emergence of the British Coffehouse* (2005), as serious centers for learning. In fact, in one case at least, that of James Jones of Southwark, a coffeehouse was used as a headquarters for church-planting.

Before Benjamin Keach came to London in 1668 and became the leading figure among the Southwark Baptists on the south side of the Thames River—Keach was pastor of the congregation that many years later worshiped at the Metropolitan Tabernacle—James Jones was the major Baptist pastor in this area of the capital. Jones had been trained as a tailor, but later Baptist tradition knew him as the "coffee-man in Southwark." He was so named due to his ownership of a coffeehouse in the parish of St. Olave, Southwark, from which he sought to lead his congregation and plant others. At the height of his ministry in the 1670s and 1680s he had, it appears, at least three different locales where he met with fellow believers for worship and the preaching of the Word.

Imprisoned for worship
This was a difficult era, however, for any who sought to be involved in churches apart from the Church of England. The restoration of the monarchy in 1660—after the tumult of the British civil wars and the republican government of the 1650s—had seen the enacting of a body of legislation known now as the Clarendon Code. It led to serious persecution of those who dissented from the state church, many of whom ended up paying substantial fines or experiencing life-threatening imprisonment. The final years of Charles II's reign in the 1680s witnessed an intensification of the persecution of these Dissenters. During this period nearly 4,000 London

Dissenters were arrested or convicted for being present at what the state regarded as illegal religious meetings. A group of thuggish informers known as the Hilton gang terrorized London Dissenters, spying on their worship services, reporting them to the authorities, participating in their prosecution, and seizing their property if they could.

Among those arrested in 1682 was James Jones. His crime was participation in illegal worship and for not attending worship in the state church. Jones' arrest and subsequent imprisonment seems to have been a key event that led to a flurry of literary activity in which he published a series of small tracts in defence of religious liberty, including *The Grand Case of Subjection to the Higher Powers, in Matters of Religion Resolved* (1684), *Nonconformity Not Inconsistent with Loyalty* (1684), and *A Plea for Liberty of Conscience* (1684).

Pleading for religious liberty

In these works Jones argued that he and other Dissenters could not conform to the Church of England because they failed to find such a national, state church in the New Testament. What they did find were "congregational churches" under the rule of "pastors, elders, and overseers." Moreover, state compulsion in the matter of religion fundamentally misunderstood the nature of the Christian Faith because the "conformity [compelled] is to man and not to God" and is a "ready way to make men hypocrites." It is noteworthy that Jones did not bear ill-will against those genuine Christians who conformed to the Anglican state church. As Jones put it, "the Protestant Dissenters have a great veneration and high esteem of many both of the nobility, gentry, clergy, and common people of the Church of England, who live sober lives and walk conscientiously in civil and religious matters."

The Glorious Revolution of 1688/1689, when the Roman Catholic monarch James II was replaced by the Protestants William III and Mary II, brought a genuine measure of religious freedom. It would appear, though, that Jones did not live to see it. His coffeehouse, however, continued to be used in the 1690s as a meeting–place for Baptist leaders. Here pastors like Benjamin Keach, Hercules Collins, and Joseph Stennett enjoyed fellowship as well as mutual encouragement and support in the oversight of their

London Baptist congregations.

And thus, coffee played a role in the dissemination of gospel truth in late seventeenth-century Britain. Maybe there is material here for a study of the theological life of coffee!

38

The hymns of Isaac Watts and
the conversion of George Thomson

George Thomson was the Anglican vicar of St. Gennys, a windswept village in North Cornwall perched atop cliffs overlooking the Atlantic. Though an ordained minister in the Church of England, Thomson had come to St. Gennys with little interest, if any, in spiritual matters, and was one whose life was characterized by "debaucheries" of various sorts. He was typical of far too many Anglican ministers of that day.

Awakened by a dream

In 1733 or 1734 Thomson was awakened from his benighted state by a dream, which was repeated three times in one night with ever-increasing terror. In the first instance of the dream, he was told: "This day month, at six in the afternoon, you must appear before the judgment seat of Christ, to give an account of the dreadful abuse of all your talents, and the injuries done the souls committed to your care." Thomson woke in alarm, but soon shrugged off the dream with the thought, "Glad I am it was no more than a dream; I am no old woman to mind dreams," and promptly fell back asleep. The dream was repeated "with greater circumstances of terror," and Thomson awoke again, this time deeply shaken. After much tossing and agitation, he was able to go back to sleep once more, only to be awakened after the dream had been repeated yet a third time.

Now terrified and convinced that he had but a month to live, Thomson called together his friends and the leading individuals in the parish. He recounted his dream to them, told them to find someone to fill the pulpit, and to return to conduct his funeral in a month.

An evangelical conversion

Thomson then shut himself up in his home and for two weeks was in deep despair, since he was persuaded that it was not consistent with God's honour for him to forgive one who had brought such dishonour upon his holy name. After a fortnight of such distress, however, Thomson was led by the Spirit of

123

God to read Romans 3, where he clearly saw that God could be glorified in his salvation, through the propitiation of Christ's most precious blood.

Thomson returned to his pulpit and began to preach those doctrines which in a few years would be the hallmark of the Evangelical Revival: the atoning death of Christ and the imputation of his righteousness, the necessity of the new birth, and the absolute need of the Holy Spirit's power and presence to begin and carry on a saving change in heart and life.

Watts' hymns: a means of grace

Soon after his conversion Thomson discovered the hymns of a certain well-known hymnwriter, who, through the medium of his hymns became something of a spiritual mentor to Thomson. The well-known hymnwriter was none other than Isaac Watts.

Writing to Watts in 1736, Thomson said:

> Poet, Divine, Saint, the delight, the guide the wonder of the virtuous world; permit, Reverend Sir, a stranger unknown, and likely to be for ever unknown, to desire one blessing from you in a private way. 'Tis this, that when you approach the Throne of Grace, and lift up holy hands, when you get closest to the Mercy-seat, and wrestle mightily for the peace of Jerusalem, you would breathe one petition for my soul's health. In return I promise you a share for life in my unworthy prayers, who honour you as a father and a brother (though differently ordered) and conclude myself,
> Your affectionate humble Servant, George Thomson.

It must have been something of a surprise to Watts to have received this "gushing" letter of adulation from an Anglican minister. Thomson's remark about his being "differently ordered" reflects the difference in church communion between writer and recipient: Watts was a Dissenter and Thomson an Anglican. As such, the effusive, and by our standards far too flowery, praise that Thomson lavishes on Watts is particularly noteworthy.

In fact, Thomson confesses, Watts' hymns were the medium by which God made him a "father" and mentor in the Christian life for the Anglican vicar. Thomson was not the only one Watts mentored through his hymns. Countless others who have sung Watts' hymns have blessed God for the life of this brother in Christ and his hymns. For Thomson, Watts' hymns were nothing less than a means of grace.

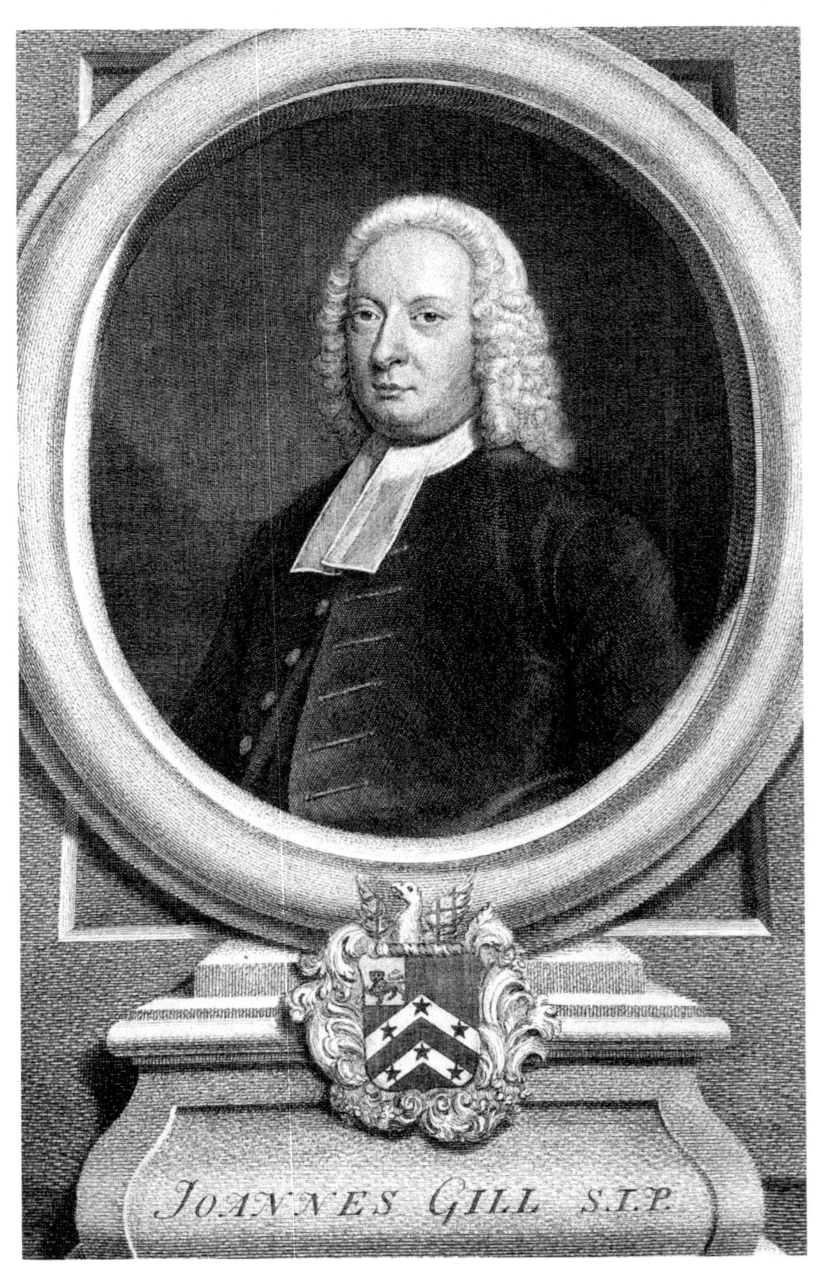

John Gill

39

John Gill comes to London

From time to time in the history of the Church, God raises up men, who, because of their God-given talents, exercise extraordinary influence for good. In the Ancient Church Athanasius and Augustine were such pastor-theologians as they defended the Christian Faith. At the time of the Reformation, Martin Luther and John Calvin were critical to the advance of that great move of God. And in more recent days, D. Martyn Lloyd-Jones played a central role in the recovery of the doctrines of grace among Anglophone Evangelicals. And in his day, especially among members of his community, the Particular or Calvinistic Baptists, John Gill may rightly be reckoned, in the words of Lloyd-Jones, "a very great man, and an exceptionally able man."

Gill viewed negatively

Yet, contrary to this perspective, Gill has been remembered by many as a hyper-Calvinist whose theology has been seen as a major cause for the decline of his Baptist denomination for much of the eighteenth century. By the time that the Victorian Baptist historian J.M. Cramp, for instance, came to write his influential and widely-read *Baptist History*, the responsibility of Gill for the decline of the Baptist cause in the eighteenth century was a given.

Gill "abstained from personal addresses to sinners, by inviting them to the Saviour." Instead, he was content "with stating men's danger, and assuring them they were on the high road to perdition." When his teaching was embraced by many in the Baptist community, Cramp was not surprised that their churches experienced declension.

In the middle of the twentieth century, historian A.C. Underwood reiterated the charge: despite his great learning, Gill "never addressed the ungodly" in his preaching. On the other side of the Atlantic, Southern Baptist historian H. Leon McBeth likewise opined in a massive study of Baptist history that Gill's "hyper-Calvinism" with its "rigid "non-invitation" style of theology and preaching, while ringing with impressive logic, brought the kiss of death" to the Calvinistic Baptists.

Gill defending the Trinity

This perspective on Gill has a good deal of truth in it, but, like so many other figures in church history, Gill's legacy is complex. While his theology did contain definite elements of hyper-Calvinism, it was also a bastion against the destructive forces unleashed during the eighteenth century by what is called the Enlightenment, which exalted the omnicompetence of human reason. In the crosshairs of many of the rationalistic protagonists of the Enlightenment was the central Christian truth of the doctrine of the Trinity.

Some Christian communities, like the English Presbyterians, largely succumbed to this attack on the Trinity, but not so the Particular Baptists—and that largely because of John Gill. This Baptist theologian stood firm for the doctrine of the Trinity that had been hammered out in the fourth century and codified in what came to be called the Nicene Creed. This creedal statement declared Christ to be fully God since he shared the very being of God and all of his divine attributes to the full. The Spirit was also fully divine since he was worshipped and glorified with the Father and the Son.

Gill's written works, including a powerful study of the Trinity, came to be possessed by most Baptist pastors. By standing squarely for this vital doctrine, Gill thus enabled his Baptist contemporaries to maintain their hold on orthodoxy and so have the capacity to receive the fire of revival later in the century.

Gill comes to London

Gill was in the position to exercise such influence since he was the pastor of one of the largest and most important Baptist congregations in London, which met at Goat Yard, Horselydown. When its pastor, Benjamin Stinton, had died unexpectedly in February of 1719, Gill was invited to preach in the summer of 1719. This preaching engagement led to Gill being invited to preach for the whole month of August, during which time a goodly number of the church clearly came to the conviction that they had found their new pastor in this twenty-one year old who hailed from Northamptonshire.

A church meeting was held on Sunday, September 13, 1719, to vote on calling Gill. The motion passed "by a very great majority." While there was significant opposition by the deacons of the church to calling Gill, he came to London as the pastor of this church in 1719. And in the providence of God, it was good that he did, for he and his books would be critical in preserving the orthodoxy of the Particular, or Calvinistic Baptists.

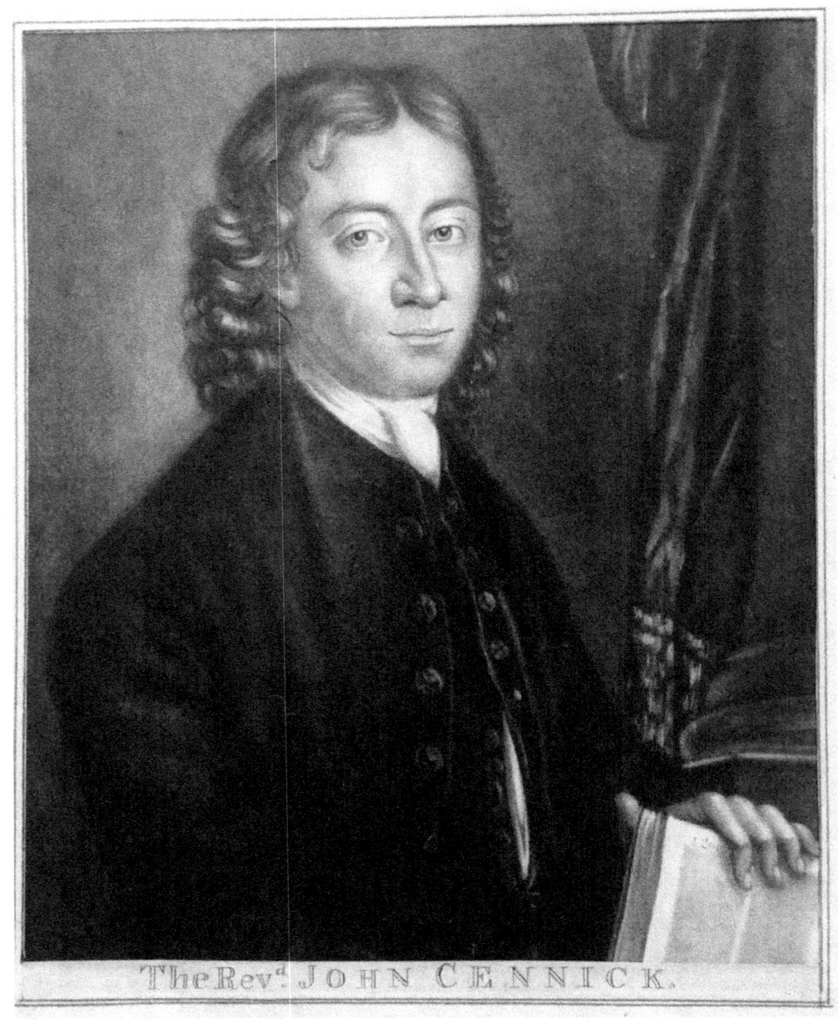

John Cennick

40
"Moravianism at its loveliest and best": Remembering John Cennick

Some of the eras of Church History are clearly more momentous than others: the fourth century, for example, saw the resolution of the Arian controversy with the landmark statement of the Nicene Creed; the sixteenth century witnessed the massive recovery of Gospel truth; and the eighteenth century saw the transatlantic revivals that laid the foundations for modern Evangelicalism.

Now, among those who were vitally used in the establishment of Evangelical roots was the Moravian evangelist John Cennick. Though largely unknown today to all but students of the eighteenth-century Evangelical awakenings in the British Isles, in his day he preached (and prayed) with such Evangelical celebrities as John and Charles Wesley, George Whitefield, and Howell Harris, and was well regarded by these men. In the words of Arnold Dallimore: Cennick "was not only one of the greatest preachers of the 18th Century Revival but also one of its greatest saints. In him Moravianism is seen at its loveliest and best."

By the way, as Gary M. Best has noted in a biography of the evangelist, the first letter of his family name is probably best pronounced as a "K," thus "Kennick."

Conversion from legalism and libertinism
Cennick grew up in a legalistic Anglican setting, where his mother insisted that he spend the Lord's Day reading or saying hymns. Not surprisingly he rebelled against this upbringing in his teen years and immersed himself in card-playing, dancing, and gambling at the race-track. In 1735, though—the very year in which his fellow evangelists Howell Harris and George Whitefield were converted—he was smitten with a deep sense of his guilty state. At times he sought flight from his fears of judgment in atheism. At other times, Luther-like, he thought he should join a monastery and to prepare for a monastic regimen of purging his soul he took to eating only grass and acorns!

Deliverance came in September of 1737, when, in the midst of an Anglican prayer service, Cennick heard the words Psalm 34:19 ("Great are the troubles of the righteous: but the Lord delivereth him out of all" [*Book of Common Prayer*]). He realized that his spiritual destitution was being described and that there was mercy available for even he. "My heart danced for joy," he later wrote in his diary—"I heard the voice of Jesus, saying, I am thy salvation."

Neither Wesleyan nor Calvinist

Over the course of the next two years Cennick met Whitefield and John Wesley, became Methodism's first lay preacher and was deeply involved in the revival then taking place. Theological tensions, however developed between Cennick and the Wesleys when the former embraced Calvinism, and eventually there was a not-too-pleasant parting of the ways between Cennick and the Wesley brothers. It is ironic that John Wesley had a prayer written by Cennick inscribed on his teapot: "Be present at our table, Lord; be here, and everywhere adored; thy creatures bless, and grant that we may feast in Paradise with thee."

For a while, from 1741 to 1744, Cennick worked alongside the Calvinist Whitefield as his leading assistant, but this also came to an end in 1745 when he joined the Moravians, a small but remarkable body of evangelistic Christians who were based in Germany and who were a catalyst for revival in that era.

Called to preach in Ireland

As a Moravian preacher Cennick travelled throughout the British Isles, especially knowing God's blessing in Ireland. Some Dublin Baptists who had heard Cennick preach were so inspired by his sermons that they begged him to visit Ireland. At first, Cennick was not interested. As he later admitted, he had "a strong prejudice against the whole Irish nation and people."

During a trip to the Moravian heartland on the continent, though, Cennick could not get the needs of Ireland out of his mind. Eventually, he sailed to Ireland in early June 1746, praying that the Lord would stand by him in "this strange country." He would be the first of the great evangelists of that era to go to the Irish.

41

Being Anne Steele

Sadly forgotten today, the Baptist authoress Anne Steele has been rightly called the "mother of the English hymn," and to the close of the nineteenth century was as famous as Isaac Watts, John Newton, or William Cowper. She was the daughter of William Steele, the pastor of the Particular Baptist chapel in Broughton, Hampshire, a village situated roughly mid-way between Salisbury and Winchester. Converted in 1732 and baptized the same year, she grew to be a woman of deep piety, genuine cheerfulness and blessed with a mind hungry for knowledge. Her piety was wrought in the furnace of affliction. She wrestled most of her adult life, it appears, with ongoing bouts of tertian malaria and terrible stomach pain.

She never married, although there were two proposals of marriage—one from none other than the Baptist pastor and hymnwriter Benjamin Beddome. Anne, however, made a conscious choice to remain single. In a letter she wrote to her step-sister after refusing one of these proposals, she said that the suitor had offered his hand to help over the stile, that is, get married. But when she looked over into the meadow of marriage, she wrote:

> I looked over and saw no flowers, but observ'd a great many thorns, and I suppose there are more hid under the leaves, but as there is not verdure enough to cover half of 'em it must be near winter, as I think it generally happens when I look into the said Meadow.

So, Anne remained single. But her singleness gave her the time to devote herself to poetry and hymn-writing, a gift with which the Lord had richly blessed her. About ten years before her death, sixty-two of her hymns were published in a Baptist hymnal entitled *A Collection of Hymns Adapted to Public Worship* (1769), whose editors were John Ash and Caleb Evans. This hymnal gave her hymns a wide circulation throughout Baptist circles and played a critical role in the revival of the Baptist cause in England at the close of the eighteenth century.

133

The impact and theology of her hymns

One of the very few of her hymns that is still sung today reveals the way in which this wide circulation of her hymns would have played a part in revitalizing areas of the Particular Baptist cause. It was originally entitled "The Savior's Invitation," and was based on Jesus' words in John 7:37, "If any man thirst, let him come unto me, and drink" (KJV).

> The Saviour calls—let every Ear
> Attend the heavenly Sound;
> Ye doubting Souls, dismiss your Fear,
> Hope smiles reviving round.
>
> For every thirsty, longing Heart,
> Here Streams of Bounty flow,
> And Life, and Health, and Bliss impart,
> To banish mortal Woe.
>
> Here, Springs of sacred Pleasure rise
> To ease your every Pain,
> (Immortal Fountain! full Supplies!)
> Nor shall you thirst in vain.
>
> Ye Sinners come, 'tis Mercy's Voice,
> The gracious Call obey;
> Mercy invites to heavenly Joys,—
> And can you yet delay?
>
> Dear Savior, draw reluctant Hearts,
> To Thee let Sinners fly;
> And take the Bliss Thy Love imparts,
> And drink, and never die.

Based on Jesus' open invitation to sinners to come to him and drink, that is, find eternal life, Steele urges "every Ear" to "attend" to Christ's heavenly invitation. He calls all who are "thirsty" and "longing" to come to him, where they will find "Life, and Health, and Bliss," in sum, "Springs of sacred Pleasure" that will ease every woe. This invitation is a command—"the gracious Call obey"—and a free offer—"can you yet delay?"

But Steele is also aware that the "thirsty, longing Heart" is not sufficient in itself to come to Christ. In the final analysis it is a "reluctant Heart," filled with doubt and fear. Hence, she prays, "Dear Savior, draw reluctant hearts." And this is a prayer that can be prayed with confidence, for the Saviour to whom she speaks is an "Immortal Fountain," Mercy incarnate who loves sinners and delights in bestowing on them "heavenly joys."

As Particular Baptist men and women sang this hymn, it was preparing them for the revival that came to their community in the final decades of the eighteenth century. Oh, that this were true of our hymnody today!

42

Loving the lost:
following the example of Jonathan Edwards

When Jonathan Edwards, who has been rightly described as "America's Augustine," left his pastoral charge in Northampton, Massachusetts, in 1750, he received a number of "attractive" ministry offers, including the presidency of a theological college in Scotland. He chose instead to go with his family to a small out-of-the-way frontier village by the name of Stockbridge, Massachusetts. Why this unusual choice?

Some have surmised that Edwards settled in Stockbridge because the rigours of ministry among a smaller congregation, which consisted mostly of Mahican Indians, would prove minimal, and he could then devote himself largely to his study and the major treatises that he wanted to write, books on such issues as free will and original sin. In other words, some have viewed Edwards in Stockbridge almost like an academic scholar on an extended sabbatical! Samuel Hopkins, in his important memoir of his mentor, seems to imply something like this when he states that God gave Edwards "a quiet retreat" at Stockbridge where he could pursue his writing. This view has been furthered by the belief that Edwards simply preached rehashed sermons from his Northampton years.

An initial clue as to why Edwards came to Stockbridge is found in the geographical location of the home in which Jonathan Edwards and his family lived during their sojourn in Stockbridge from 1751 to 1757. The house has been long gone, though its location is marked today by a sundial. Edwards purposely located it among the Mahican Indians of the town. Edwards was making a clear statement, namely, that he had genuinely come to minister to these people. It is noteworthy in this regard that his son Jonathan Jr. would later recall that his boyhood friends were all Indians and that he never spoke English outside of the family circle.

Edwards' large correspondence from this period of his life also reveals that his pre-eminent goal was to reach the Native Americans with the life-giving gospel. And his sermons from this period show that the majority of them were not simply repeats of sermons that he had preached in

Northampton, but brand-new sermons constructed with careful attention to the audience to whom they were to be preached and the end to which they were intended.

Edwards had a great desire to see the world-wide advance of the kingdom of Christ and he was convinced that the conversion of the peoples of North America had a place in this advance. The life of David Brainerd and his work among the first peoples of America would influence Edwards' thinking in this regard as he edited and published the life and diary of this eminent example of genuine missionary piety. Edwards had thus maintained an interest in the success of the Stockbridge mission over the years and had persuaded his Northampton congregation to heavily invest in the work during the 1740s.

This focus of Edwards' Stockbridge years, though, has not been appreciated until very recently, clear evidence of which is the fact that up until 1999 not one of the sermons that he preached to the Stockbridge Indians had been published. A number of these sermons are now available in a volume of Edwards' sermons covering the years 1743 to 1758, volume 25 in the multi-volume critical edition of Edwards' works published by Yale University Press. They reveal Edwards as a missionary preacher who was able to communicate plainly and effectively in his new evangelistic sphere.

Next week, we shall have the opportunity to look at one of these sermons and listen as Edwards preached the gospel to a group of Mohawk chiefs.

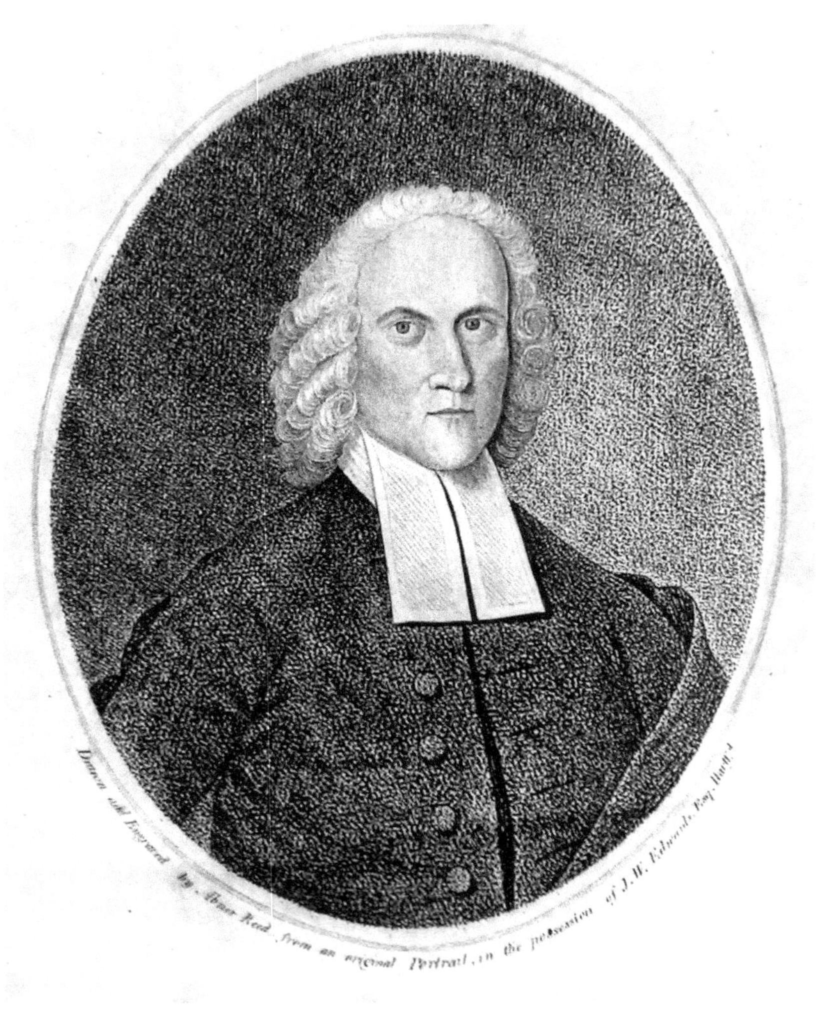

Jonathan Edwards

43

Jonathan Edwards: a theologian of love

Often when people think of Jonathan Edwards as a preacher, his famous 1741 Enfield sermon "Sinners in the hands of an angry God" is what first comes to mind. But the reality is that Edwards preached more often on heaven. His sermon "Heaven, a world of love," preached a few years before the Enfield sermon, was actually more typical of Edwards' sermonic corpus. He was, as a number of books on Edwards have recently emphasized, pre-eminently a theologian of love. His concern for the salvation and welfare of native Americans in Massachusetts is another good example of this focus.

On August 16, 1751, Edwards delivered a sermon to a group of Mohawks in Albany, New York. The Mohawks had come to Albany to discuss with Edwards what might be entailed in sending their children to a school in Stockbridge. After the discussions, Edwards was given an opportunity to preach to them. He began by stating that "when God first made man, he had a principle of holiness in his heart," like a light shining within him. But then the man sinned against God and he "lost his holiness." The light that he had was "put out" and his mind became full of darkness. The long-term result was idolatry: the worship of heavenly bodies, "images of gold and silver, brass and iron, wood and stone," animals and even the devil.

But God had mercy on mankind and gave them the Scriptures, "as a light shining in a dark place." Then Christ came to "die for sinners" and give further instruction. And so, the Bible was completed. Christ gave clear instruction that the Bible and the Gospel were to be taught to all the nations. Those nations that now have the Bible "enjoy light," while those nations without it "live in great darkness."

Edwards now spoke plainly: the forefathers of the Mohawk "have for a great many ages lived in great darkness." The Europeans, who had the Scriptures and should have taught the Native Americans, have not helped them: "They have not done their duty to you," he told his hearers, "they have greatly neglected you," and that neglect was shameful. The "white people have not behaved like Christians," for if they had, Edwards continued, they would have given the Indians the Scriptures and so shown love for their souls.

In fact, many of the "English and the Dutch" wanted to keep the Natives "in the dark for the sake of making a gain" of them and their lands. Here Edwards clearly drew upon the thinking of his grandfather Stoddard who had made similar charges nearly thirty years earlier. He also drew upon his long ministry in Northampton where he had been publicly critical of those who lived for material gain—some of whom were his own relatives. Such a life, Edwards believed, was positively dangerous to the soul.

Edwards then urged his Mohawk hearers: "Don't content yourselves to live in darkness any longer." He pleaded, "We invite you to come and enjoy the light of the Word of God." If they did, this light would shine into their hearts and change them and make them like Christ, just as "when you hold a glass out in the light of the sun, the glass will shine with a resemblance of the sun's brightness."

Though simple in language and structure, this is nevertheless a powerful presentation of the gospel. There is little doubt that this Stockbridge sermon reveals a true missionary heart. Interestingly enough, the whole sermon revolves around the theme of light, which had also dominated his earlier brilliant depiction of the world to come, "Heaven, a world of love."

American historian Ronald Story has noted that, for Edwards, "light connotes sight and insight, brightness and illumination ... something of "sweetness" and even rapture." Edwards' use of the imagery of light bespoke a heart of love for those Mohawks. We hope that some, if not all, of those Mohawks on that long-ago day on the American frontier embraced the light offered so freely to them by "America's Augustine."

44

"The most pleasing color":
Jonathan Edwards on the typology of green

In his tract, *On the three days*, the Augustinian theologian of the twelfth century, Hugh of St. Victor pursued an investigation firmly founded on the Pauline dictum of Romans 1:20 that through the visible things of creation the invisible Creator can be discerned to some degree. The beauty of colour, for instance, bespeaks a beautiful Creator: "the ruby-red roses, dazzlingly white lilies, the purple violets, in all of which not only their beauty but also their origin is marvellous—for how does God's wisdom produce such beauty from the dust of the earth?" But, Hugh continued, "green is the most beautiful colour of all" for it represents both new life in nature and the resurrection of the dead.

The world of nature: charged with God's beauty
Living in a world quite different from that of Hugh's twelfth-century Parisian Abbey of St. Victor, the New England divine of the long eighteenth century, Jonathan Edwards, was nevertheless a kindred spirit, for he too regarded the natural beauty of the world as reflective of the Triune Creator's beauty. Similar to Hugh of St. Victor, Edwards was convinced that

> the easiness and naturalness of trees and vines [are] shadows of his [i.e. God's] infinite beauty and loveliness; the crystal rivers and murmuring streams have the footsteps of his sweet grace and bounty. When we behold the light and brightness of the sun, the golden edges of an evening cloud, or the beauteous bow, we behold the adumbrations of his glory and goodness; and the blue skies, of his mildness and gentleness. There are also many things wherein we may behold his awful majesty: in the sun in his strength, in comets, in thunder, in the towering thunder clouds, in ragged rocks and the brows of mountains.

Green—"a most fit emblem of divine grace"
And like Hugh, Edwards was also certain that the colour green was the

"most pleasing" and loveliest of colours:

> This color is a most fit emblem of divine grace ... It is the color of all the grass, herbs, and trees, and growth of the earth, and therefore fitly denotes life, flourishing, prosperity, and happiness, which are often in Scripture compared to the green and flourishing growth of the earth. As the benign influence of the sun on the face of the earth is shown by this color above all others, so is the grace, and benign influence, and communication of God fitly represented by this color. This color is the color of joy and gladness. The fields are said to shout for joy, and also to sing, by their appearing in a cheerful green.

For Edwards, green is "a most fit emblem of divine grace" because, being found in grassy meadows and trees and all things verdant, it "denotes life, flourishing, prosperity, and happiness." And just as the sun is vital to this green-filled life, so the grace of God is essential for true life, genuine human flourishing, and eternal happiness and joy.

If all of this seems quite fanciful, remember who is writing these things—the greatest theologian of American history. Moreover, do such things seem fanciful because we are out of touch with God's presence in the world of nature? And have we lost the ability to see God in that world because the world we inhabit is largely filled with digital screens and cityscapes?

45

"None of the moderns have equalled
the Moravian Brethren":
Recalling the life and ministry of David Zeisberger

When William Carey drew up his paradigm-changing book, *An Enquiry into the Obligations of Christians to Use Means for the Conversion of the Heathens* in 1792, he included a mini-history of missions. He cited examples of missionaries passionate for the expansion of the rule of Christ. In this mini-history, he referenced a remarkable missions-minded community, the Moravians. Carey's words about this eighteenth-century body of believers are tantalizingly brief but indicative of their influence upon him. When I came to evangelism and missions, Carey noted, "none of the moderns have equalled the Moravian Brethren in this good work."

At the close of the 1720s, under the leadership of Nicolaus Ludwig von Zinzendorf, a wealthy aristocrat and landowner in Saxony whose devotion to Christ dated from his early years as a child, the Moravians had experienced a powerful revival. They would later term it their Pentecost. And even as the biblical Pentecost propelled the early Church into mission, so did the Moravian Pentecost.

To the ends of the earth
From Saxony, where the Moravians were based, they sent out missionaries literally to the four corners of the earth: to the West Indies in 1732, to Greenland in 1733, to Lapland and Georgia in 1734, to Surinam in 1735, to South Africa in 1737, to Algeria in 1739, to North America, Sri Lanka and Romania in 1740, and to Persia in 1747.

In the nineteenth-century, Anglophone world Carey was lionized as the father of modern missions. He knew better: he took his inspiration from the Moravians. By Zinzendorf's death in 1760 no fewer than 226 missionaries had been sent out by this relatively tiny Christian community.

David Zeisberger

Here is one story from the early annals of these remarkable Christians. Early in 1745 a couple of Moravians were arrested by English soldiers in what is present-day New York state, but what was then the American frontier and fiercely contested territory between the British and the French in their desire to dominate North America. They were incarcerated for fifty-one days in Albany on the charge of spying for the French.

They had been seized in a Mohawk village on what is now the Mohawk River, where they were seeking to learn the Mohawk tongue. When the Governor of New York, George Clinton, examined them, he specifically asked them why they wanted to learn this language. David Zeisberger, one of the two men, replied that eventually they wanted to be able "to preach among the Indians the Gospel of our crucified Saviour, and to declare to them what we have personally experienced of his grace in our own hearts."

In the course of divine providence, Zeisberger would spend his life—he lived into his eighties—preaching a crucified Saviour in the languages of the Onondaga, Iroquois, and the Delaware. His life—now three hundred years exactly since his birth in Moravia—is an amazing model of missionary energy and passion.

The judgement of William Wilberforce

Looking back on this missions outburst, William Wilberforce, the great English evangelical politician and social reformer, could say of the Moravians at the end of this first century of the modern missionary movement: "They are a body who have perhaps excelled all mankind in solid and unequivocal proofs of the love of Christ and of ardent, active zeal in his service. It is a zeal tempered with prudence, softened with meekness and supported by a courage which no danger can intimidate and a quiet certainty no hardship can exhaust."

46

"Sweet solemnity and ardent love": Andrew Fuller and a doxological faith

In December, 1967, D. Martyn Lloyd-Jones—affectionately known to many of his day and since as simply "the Doctor," a reference to his medical degree—gave an address to what was then known as the Puritan Conference on what some might have considered an esoteric topic, namely, the teachings of a small eighteenth-century movement known as Sandemanianism. Ever a believer in the value of church history for guidance in the present, Lloyd-Jones argued that the errors of this eighteenth-century movement had much to teach his hearers, for he felt that there were far too many in contemporary Evangelical circles who were replicating the central Sandemanian error, namely that true faith can be held without deeply-felt affections.

Sandemanianism

Robert Sandeman, the Scottish theologian after whom this error is named, maintained that saving faith is "bare belief of the bare truth." Sandeman was insistent that faith becomes a work of human merit if it includes anything beyond simple assent to the truth of what God has done through Christ's death and resurrection. In a genuine desire to exalt the utter freeness of God's salvation, Sandeman sought to remove any vestige of human reasoning, willing or desiring in the matter of saving faith. Sandeman was wrongly convinced that if the actions of the will or the affections are included in saving faith, then the Reformation assertion of "faith alone" is compromised. Thus, in the Sandemanian system, saving faith is reduced to intellectual assent to the gospel proclamation about Christ.

It should occasion no surprise that many of those who embraced Sandeman's intellectualist view of faith became stunted in their Christian lives. Andrew Fuller, the Particular Baptist theologian whom Lloyd-Jones identified as the key opponent of Sandeman's thought, could admit that there were "things worthy of imitation" among the Sandemanians, such as their diligence to study the Bible and live under its authority. Yet, he said, their spirituality "resembles a rickety child, whose growth is confined to certain parts: it wants that lovely uniformity or proportion which constitutes the beauty of holiness." Christmas Evans, an influential Welsh Baptist leader and a contemporary of Fuller's, adopted Sandemanian views for a number of years in the late 1790s. He soon found himself in the grip of "a cold heart towards Christ, and his sacrifice, and the work of his Spirit" and dwelling in the "sterile regions of spiritual frost." Only with much effort and prayer was Evans thankfully freed from the grip of this cold intellectualist system.

Fuller's definitive reply to the Sandemanians

Of course, Sandemanianism did not go unopposed. A number of key eighteenth-century Evangelical leaders wrote replies and rebuttals of this system, including the Methodist leader John Wesley and William Williams of Pantycelyn, the ardent Welsh Calvinistic Methodist hymn-writer. It was Andrew Fuller, though, who drew up what many then, and now, regard as the definitive response to the system of Sandeman in his *Strictures on Sandemanianism* (1810).

Essentially Fuller argued that if faith and theological reflection really concerns only the mind, then there would be no way to distinguish genuine Christianity from nominal Christianity. A nominal Christian mentally assents to the truths of Christianity, but those truths do not grip his heart and so re-orient his affections to glory in God. The opposite of saving faith in Scripture, Fuller noted, is not "simple ignorance," which it would be if the Sandemanian view of faith were correct. Its opposite is an ignorance that has its roots in a deep-seated hatred of the true God. Christ can therefore state that unbelief rejects him because, in the words of John 3:19, "darkness is loved rather than light." Or when Ephesians 4:18 talks about the understanding of unbelievers being darkened "because of the ignorance that is in them, because of the blindness of their heart," surely, Fuller reasoned, the ignorance in view here is much more than mere lack of knowledge. Does it not entail, he asked, a deep-seated aversion to God and holy things?

But if unbelief comprises much more than ignorance, then faith and right theology must entail more than knowledge. If unbelief involves an aversion to the truth and a forthright rejection of the gospel, then faith in and reflection upon the truth must include a love for and rejoicing in the truth. True conversion is rooted in a radical change of the affections of the heart and manifest in doxological theology and a lifestyle that lives for the glory of God.

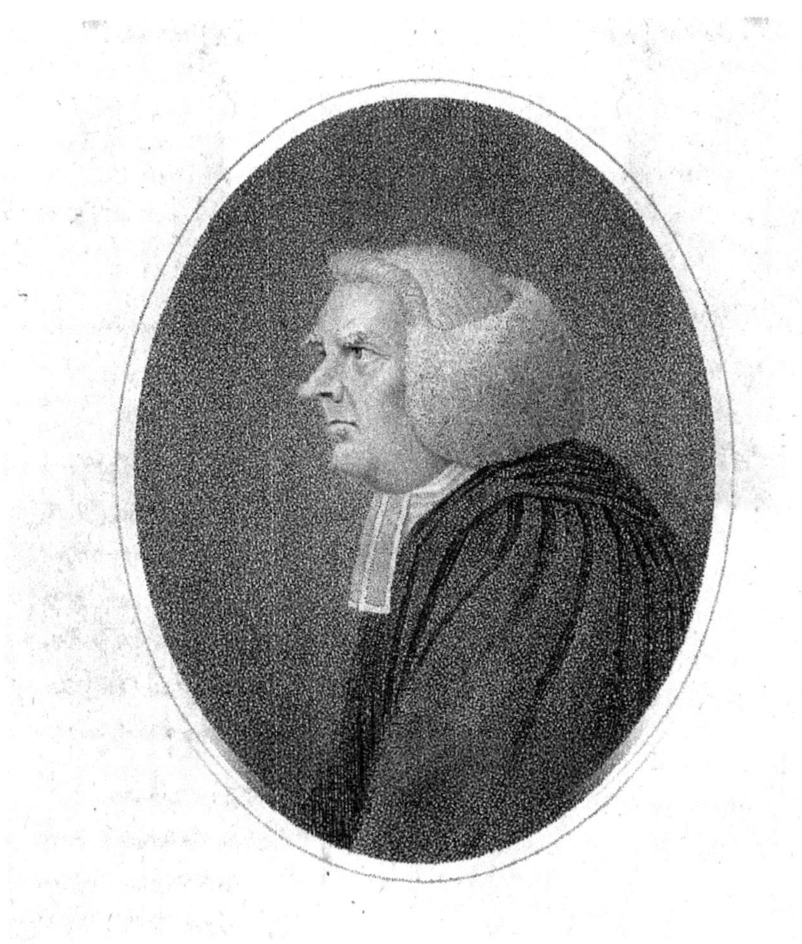

John Berridge

47

A meeting with John Berridge, the gospel pedlar

It was in the autumn of 1790, before wintry weather made the twenty miles or so between Olney, Buckinghamshire, and Everton, Bedfordshire, quite difficult for travel, that two Baptist pastors wended their way to an Anglican parish for a few hours' visit with its vicar. For much of the eighteenth century, many Baptists and Anglicans had been like the Jews and Samaritans of old: they had "no dealings" with one another (John 4:9). But times were rightly changing, and Baptists were coming to realize that it was the better part of wisdom to build friendships with gospel-centred Anglicans.

So it was that Andrew Fuller, the tall, broad-shouldered pastor of the Baptist cause in Kettering, Northamptonshire, and the author of *The Gospel Worthy of All Acceptation* (1785), which would do much to open up the Particular Baptist community to revival, along with his close friend John Sutcliff of Olney came to spend a few hours in the company of John Berridge, the vicar of St. Mary's Church, Everton. Beginning in the late 1750s, this thirteenth-century parish church had witnessed remarkable scenes of revival, when Berridge, after his own conversion in 1757, preached the gospel to literally hundreds and thousands who, like him, "fled to Jesus alone for refuge" (part of the epitaph on Berridge's tombstone in the cemetery of St. Mary's).

In the years that followed Berridge had become firmly associated with other leaders of the revival, men like George Whitefield and Henry Venn of Yelling. Like Whitefield he was a bold itinerant—a "gospel pedlar", as his recent biographer Nigel Pibworth has rightly called him. Though the frankness and directness of his pulpit ministry was considered eccentric by some—Fuller would have admired such a quality as his own preaching was similarly bold, plain and pithy—Berridge's life was also marked by what his first biographer and curate Richard Whittingham termed an "unaffected humility." Typical of Berridge are the following lines he wrote in 1773, "I am now sinking from a poor something into a vile nothing." And when he died twenty years later, he insisted on being buried in the unconsecrated ground of the church's cemetery reserved for suicides.

Berridge at prayer

What Fuller and Sutcliff remembered especially from their few hours with Berridge—at the time he was in his mid-seventies, for he had been born in 1716—was the intensity of his love to Christ and the sweetness of his praying.

When they were about to take their leave of Berridge, the three men prayed together on their knees (were they in the church at this point or Berridge's home, the seventeenth-century vicarage?). Fuller prayed first, ending his prayer with the familiar refrain, "in Christ's name." At this point, Berridge took up Fuller's prayer and began to pray, "O Lord God! This prayer has been offered up in the name of Jesus, accept it I beseech thee" and he continued on for five or six minutes with, Sutcliff later recalled, "such sweet solemnity, such holy familiarity with God, and such ardent love to Christ ... that the like was seldom seen."

The meeting's meaning

Fuller never forgot the time with Berridge, and he later reckoned it to be one of the happiest events of his life. More than that, it bespoke an important breakthrough for many Baptists like Fuller: they were realizing that while their distinctive Baptist convictions were important, they were not the sole custodians of such primary gospel truths as the new birth and regeneration by the Holy Spirit. There were others, men like Berridge, who shared their fundamental convictions, and with whom they needed to fellowship—and pray together.

Though we in the West certainly cannot be said to be enjoying the revival blessings of late eighteenth-century England, yet, the sweet fellowship that Berridge, Fuller, and Sutcliff enjoyed that autumn day in 1790 is much needed—much needed indeed!

48

A wee note of Abraham Booth and our need for gentleness

In recent days, I have been impressed with the significance of a name that was well-known among British evangelicals in the last decades of the long eighteenth century, but today is mostly forgotten, namely, that of Abraham Booth, who is not to be confused with the famous founder of the Salvation Army, William Booth.

Booth's life in brief

The son of a Nottinghamshire farmer, Booth became a stocking weaver in his teens. He had no formal schooling and was compelled to teach himself to read and to write. His early Christian experience was spent among the General, i.e. Arminian Baptists, but by 1768 he had undergone a complete revolution in his soteriology and had become a Calvinist. Not long after this embrace of Calvinism he wrote *The Reign of Grace, from Its Rise to Its Consummation* (1768), which the twentieth-century Scottish theologian John Murray regarded as "one of the most eloquent and moving expositions of the subject of divine grace in the English language."

It was this book which opened the way for his call to Prescot Street Baptist Church in what was then a wealthy area of London, home to merchants and professional men. Pastoring this church was a challenge to a man who had limited educational opportunities. Booth, though, more than rose to the challenge, in time mastering Greek, Latin, and French, the first two taught to him by a Roman Catholic priest.

It was at Prescot Street that Booth preached one of his most stirring sermons, *Commerce in the Human Species, and the Enslaving of Innocent Persons, inimical to the Laws of Moses and the Gospel of Christ*. Preached on January 29, 1792, this sermon was long remembered as a key sermon in Baptist involvement in the fight to abolish both slavery and the slave trade. Booth's fellow Londoner and Baptist Joseph Ivimey noted that Thomas Clarkson, a key abolitionist, considered it one of the most important documents in the early stages of the anti-slavery movement.

By the time of his death in 1806 Booth was one of the most trusted counsellors in the Particular Baptist denomination. His congregation genuinely adored him for what contemporaries called his "unsullied purity and kindliness." One of them penned a most moving, though brief, tribute in the church minute book after his death: "He sought not ours, but us."

"Oh for the meekness and gentleness of Christ!"
A friend of mine passed along to me a transcription of one of Booth's letters that he had come across in a nineteenth-century religious magazine. There are few of Booth's letters extant, and this letter is a gem. In reality, it is more of a wee note than a letter. It is a text that could have easily been tossed out, but it was preserved by the recipient for decades after she had received it.

It was written on August 26, 1805, but five months before Booth's death. The note was written to a female member of his congregation, to whom, it appears, he had been rather sharp the previous day when speaking with her.

> My Christian Friend,
> I take the first opportunity of acknowledging that, in my treatment of you yesterday, there were some improprieties, which, on reflection, I cannot but condemn, and on account of which I am very sorry. Oh for *the meekness and gentleness of Christ!* But, as I mean to take an early opportunity of calling upon you, I conclude, and remain,
> My Christian friend,
> Your unworthy pastor,
> Abraham Booth.

August 26 in 1805 was a Monday, and thus it was on the Lord's day, August 25, that Booth sinned in his speech against this sister. He was a mature Christian by this point in time, yet, as we see in this note, very conscious of the fact that there is never a moment in the believer's life when grace and gentleness are not needed.

PLAIN

CHRISTIAN DUTIES,

RECOMMENDED,

IN AN EXHORTATION,

delivered at the Settlement of a Church,

Of the Baptist Denomination.

On the 22d. of March 1791,

and now published

(by request)

FOR THE BENEFIT OF

CHRISTIANS in GENERAL,

AND

MEMBERS of CHURCHES

IN PARTICULAR

———————————————

BY ZENAS TRIVETT.

———————————————

" Let all things be done decently, and in order."

" Only let your conversation be as it becometh the gospel of Christ."

PAUL.

✻ ✻ ✻

S U D B U R Y:

printed by

W. BRACKETT,

and sold by J. F. & C. RIVINGTONS, London;

and

may be had of the AUTHOR.

M,DCCXCI.

PRICE SIXPENCE.

The title page of Zenas Trivett, *Plain Christian Duties Recommended*

156

49

Remembering Zenas Trivett

During the global pandemic in 2020, I was asked to write an introduction for a book by a little-known Baptist minister named Zenas Trivett. Entitled *Plain Christian Duties Recommended*, it is an address that Trivett gave at the establishment of a new Baptist congregation in 1791—we are not told where, though it was probably in Essex where Trivett's pastorate was located at Langham. This small pamphlet lays out the various responsibilities of a faithful member of a local church. Not surprisingly, Trivett emphasized that congregational polity was "the alone [i.e. only] plan of the New Testament," though he urged his hearers never to dream that "all true religion [is] confined to your own denomination." He particularly urged the congregation to often "meet together … for prayer and conversation." For often believers who had come together "destitute of the spirit of devotion," Trivett noted, have "had their cold affections warmed."

Being Zenas Trivett

But who was Zenas Trivett? In an anonymous obituary that was written for him after his death, the author of the obituary indicated his desire for any of his readers who could write "a more prolonged memoir" than he had done, to do so. Sadly, none was forthcoming. The materials we have then for even a small biographical sketch like this are sparse at best.

Trivett grew up in the robust Baptist work in Worstead, Norfolk, where his father Edward Trivett was the pastor of the church for many years. Converted in 1775 and baptized in May of that year, Zenas began to preach the following year. One of his many converts whose name we know was a woman named Esther Rogers, who was saved in 1776 through a sermon that he preached on Revelation 6:17 ("The great day of his wrath is come" [KJV]) at Eythorne, Kent. Two years later, in 1778, he assumed the pastorate of the Baptist church in Langham, Essex, which he pastored for forty years till his retirement in 1819. Ten years after Trivett retired from Langham, the congregation numbered around 450, the bulk of whom had been added during Trivett's ministry.

With his good friend Thomas Stevens of Colchester, Trivett was involved in the formation of the Essex Baptist Association in 1796, which provided a vehicle for church planting and revitalization in the county. Prior to this, his church had been involved in the Norfolk and Suffolk Association. Trivett continued to attend the annual meetings of the Norfolk and Suffolk Association after the formation of the Essex Association. Trivett was also a strong supporter of the Bristol Baptist Academy and the Baptist Missionary Society, and was a signatory at the meeting that set up the first Baptist Union in 1812. His involvement in these various endeavours brought him into the circle of Baptist leaders associated with Andrew Fuller, John Ryland, Jr., and Thomas Steevens. Fuller met Trivett on a number of occasions and treasured his friendship.

Trivett appears to have published only two works: a broadsheet entitled *A Scheme of Chronology representing at one View, the Times of the Prophets, and how long they Prophesied* (1794) and the sermon mentioned earlier.

A good day

Very few details of his ministry have come down to us, although we do know that from November 10 to 17, 1802, Trivett played a large public role in the opening of a Baptist church building in Thorpe-le-Soken that still stands and the ordination of this church's first pastor, a Mr. W. Bolton. The church was formally opened for worship on November 10 and that Lord's Day, November 14, Trivett preached what was described as "an impressive discourse" from Philippians 1:27. Bolton was ordained the following Wednesday, November 17, and Trivett again gave an address. In the record of the ordination service that we have, it was said to have been "a good day."

Indeed, whenever, the church sends forth workers into the harvest and so helps to answer the prayer of Matthew 9:38, it is a good day!

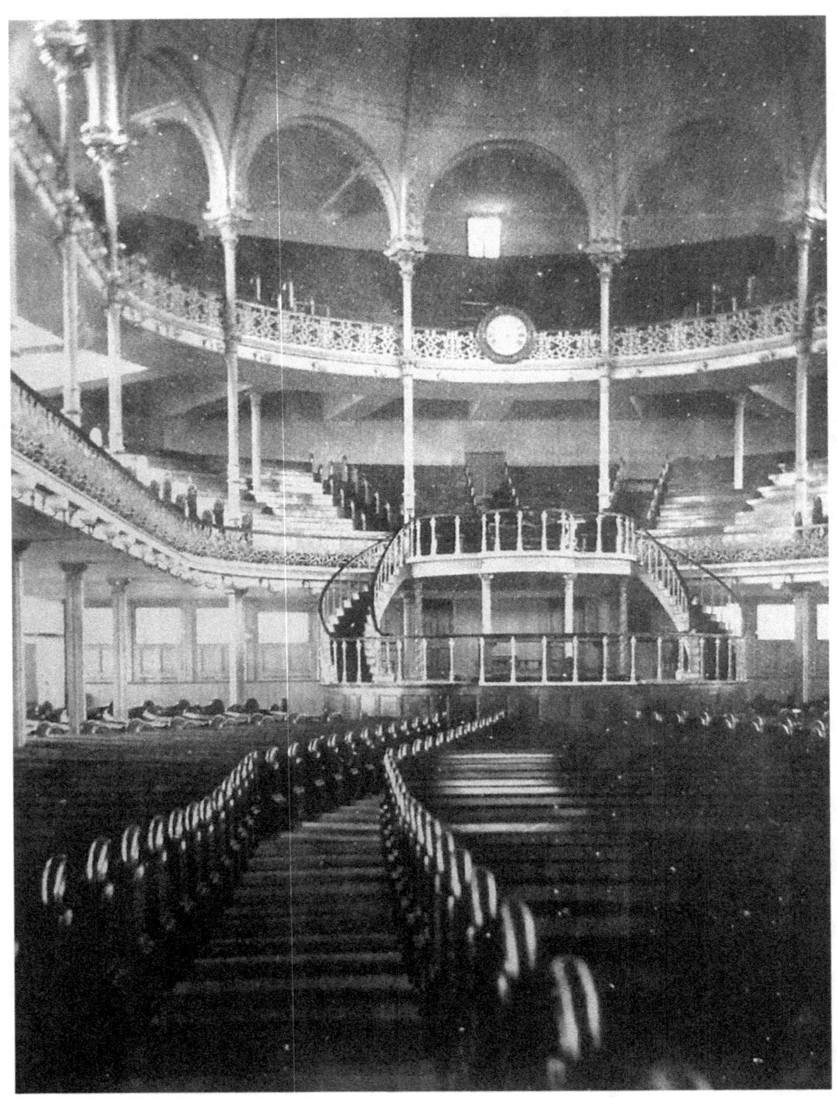

The earliest known photo of the interior of the Metropolitan Tabernacle, taken in 1861. From *The Metropolitan Tabernacle and Its Institutions* (London: Passmore and Alabaster, 1882), 3. The photo is called "East view from the Gallery." Thanks to T.D. Hale for providing the author and publisher with this picture.

50

"The main want of the Church is the Spirit": listening afresh to C.H. Spurgeon

Far too many communities of contemporary Western Evangelicals are in a parlous state: some are captive to right-wing political ideologies (especially in the United States); others, if the truth be told, are dubious about any real success of the Gospel in a secular state; while yet others are being consumed by faddishness in their pursuit of being relevant. All of these various groups, indeed all of us, desperately need to realize our great need of the Holy Spirit, without whom we can do nothing of real spiritual value and without whom we can never hope to flourish. And here the Victorian preacher C.H. Spurgeon can help us enormously.

The necessity of the Spirit

During 1859, when a powerful revival swept through much of Great Britain, Spurgeon preached a series of sermons on what are sometimes referred to as "the five points of Calvinism." He was firmly convinced that the proclamation of these doctrines would help further the revival that was then underway. One of these sermons, entitled "The Necessity of the Spirit's Work," began by sketching the Biblical teaching on men and women outside of Christ: they are dead in sin, "utterly and entirely averse to everything that is good and right," totally unwilling to come to Christ. Only the Spirit, Spurgeon averred, can remedy this situation; he alone can change the will, "correct the bias of the heart," set men and women on the right road and "give [them] strength to run in it."

When Spurgeon turned to examine the means by which the Spirit brings men and women to Christ—for instance, the preaching of the Word—and the means by which he takes them on to maturity—for example, baptism and the Lord's Supper—he found that all of these means are completely inadequate unless the Spirit deigns to use them. Indeed, Spurgeon stressed, until the Spirit calls the unbeliever out of darkness into the light of God's kingdom, his or her "election is a dead letter."

Likewise, the redemption accomplished by the Lord Jesus is of no avail, until the Spirit applies Christ's redemptive work to the soul.

> Christ's blood and righteousness are like wine stored in the wine-vat; but we cannot get thereat. The Holy Spirit dips our vessel into this precious wine, and then we drink; but without the Spirit we must die and perish just as much, though the Father elect and the Son redeem, as though the Father had never elected, and though the Son had never bought us with his blood. The Spirit is absolutely necessary. Without him neither the works of the Father, nor of the Son, are of any avail to us.

Spurgeon concluded this sermon by stressing that the vital necessity of the Spirit's work in the believer does not come to an end at conversion, for "the acceptable acts of the Christian's life, cannot be performed without the Spirit."

"Come, Holy Spirit, come"

Four years later, preaching on Acts 2:1–4, Spurgeon again emphasized "how absolutely necessary is the presence and power of the Holy Spirit."

> It is not possible for us to promote the glory of God or to bless the souls of men, unless the Holy Ghost shall be in us and with us. Those who were assembled on that memorable day of Pentecost, were all men of prayer and faith; but even these precious gifts are only available when the celestial fire sets them on a blaze. ... [E]ven these favoured and honoured saints can do nothing without the breath of God the Holy Ghost. ... [I]f so it was with them, much more must it be the case with us. Let us beware of trusting to our well-adjusted machineries of committees and schemes; let us be jealous of all reliance upon our own mental faculties or religious vigour; let us be careful that we do not look too much to our leading preachers and evangelists, for if we put any of these in the place of the Divine Spirit, we shall err most fatally.

This absolute need of the Spirit on the part of the church and of the individual believer was a constant refrain in Spurgeon's sermons and writings over the next twenty-nine years till his death in 1892. For instance, in a sermon preached in 1864 on "The Superlative Excellence of the Holy

Spirit," he challenged his hearers:

> Do not say that we want money; we shall have it soon enough when the Spirit touches men's hearts. Do not say that we want buildings, churches, edifices; all these may be very well in subserviency, but the main want of the Church is the Spirit, and men into whom the Spirit may be poured.

Spurgeon was thus constrained to stop preaching in the middle of the sermon and pray out loud, "Come, Holy Spirit, come, we can do nothing without thee; but if we have thy wind, we spread our sail, and speed onward towards glory."

Oh that every Evangelical pulpit would pray thus and that God would be pleased to answer!

51

Remembering H.M. Gwatkin

The name of Henry Melvil Gwatkin has long been a familiar one through his standard examination of the Arian heresy, *Studies of Arianism* (1882), which remains a classical study of this ancient heresy. Gwatkin was rendered deaf as a young boy by an attack of scarlet fever, but that did not seem to have curbed his intellectual development. He had a love for history from an early age and in time developed that requisite for good historical scholarship, accuracy, which, Glover recalls, was "always his passion." This concern for accuracy gave him a wonderful knowledge of original sources. But he also had a concern for relating the past to the present—always a good quality in an historian, so preventing him or her from becoming a mere antiquarian.

His great goal in life to become a Professor of Ecclesiastical History at Cambridge University was realized in 1891 when he was appointed in this capacity as a fellow at Emmanuel College—that one-time seedbed of Puritan preachers. Here he shone as a lecturer and tutor in church history, "clear, witty, stimulating, and (when he chose) eloquent" is the way one biographical sketch put it. He also had the opportunity to provide spiritual counsel for many of the students that passed through Emmanuel's halls. The last years of his life were spent during the terrible horrors of World War I, but he never lost a sense of the fact that "Eternal Love" in Christ "is sovereign," as he put it in a letter he wrote in August 1916. That very month he was knocked down by a car that he had not heard because of his deafness. He died three months later.

Church and empire

Ten years before his death, Gwatkin published a collection of sermons entitles *The Eye for Spiritual Things And Other Sermons*. In one of them he spoke on the famous text from Isaiah 6: "In the year that king Uzziah died I saw the Lord." It was preached in Girton College on January 27, 1901, and was entitled "The Death of Queen Victoria." What powerful reverberations her death sent out to the four corners of that Empire that once ruled the waves. Gwatkin well knew and he said England stood "at the parting of the ways. The Victorian age is ended."

The sermon called its hearers to rely upon the Lord but it has a long section in which Gwatkin spoke in distinctly messianic tones of England's vocation and that of her people:

> England is as much God's people as ever Israel was, and London just as much his dwelling as Jerusalem. Our land is as holy as Judah; our streets are as near him as the mercy-seat of old. ... As he chose Israel to do one great work for him, so has he chosen England now to do another. ... It is he who has made us as the stars of heaven for number, and given us western lands and southern seas for our inheritance. It is he who made peace on our soil, hardly broken by the tread of enemies for the best part of a thousand years—he, who gave the pride of the Spaniard to the winds before us, and scattered the fleets of France in the clash at Trafalgar.

Gwatkin did note that God's love for England is not because of "England's righteousness": it "was not our own right hand—our wooden walls and streak of silver sea—that wrought salvation for us, but the Lord himself has been a wall of fire about us. Our fathers cried to him, and he delivered them in many a day of trouble and rebuke—to set our rule in the sea, and our dominion at the world's end." And the task for which God had given England safety and succour? "God never gave Israel a nobler task than he has laid on England—to witness of truth and peace and mercy to every nation under heaven."

So thought one Anglican clergyman at the height of the British Empire. Such a reading of history is not unique to the English Christians of that day. Christians in the late Roman Empire, after the Edict of Milan, also spoke in similar sacral tones of the so-called Christian Roman Empire. That God did greatly use the English to spread the gospel to the four corners of the earth in the "Protestant century," namely the nineteenth century, is undisputed fact. But as that century wore on, far too much of English mission became increasingly intermeshed with the conscious dissemination of English culture and the importance of maintaining English hegemony over other cultures. It is noteworthy that Gwatkin makes nary a mention of the Welsh, the Scots, or the Irish, as if the English were able to build their empire alone and without the other peoples of this archipelago.

Well, this Anglocentric reading of history is now history itself. God, in his mercy did secure England from the Spanish Armada and the despotism of Napoleon, but to what end? That Britannia might rule the waves? Or that English voices might proclaim the rule of King Jesus to the nations? Surely the latter. And as the twentieth century would show, after Gwatkin's death, that rule did not need English voices to continue its advance.

52

Revival and the formation of a Toronto church in 1919

During and after World War I, many English-speaking Evangelicals were hoping and praying that one positive result of the horrors of that war would be a great awakening of men and women to their sin and their need for the Saviour. It was not to be, but there were local revivals that, a century on, we should remember.

The Stephens brothers
One such revival took place in Toronto in 1919, when two itinerant American evangelists, Harold L. Stephens and his brother George, were invited to speak at Calvary Baptist Church in the east end of Toronto. They were Methodists with a theology shaped by the holiness movement of the previous century. They were particularly emphatic on the necessity of not only talking about the sins of non-Christians, but also about the sins of the saints.

Also prominent in their preaching was the person and work of the Holy Spirit, an emphasis not uncommon throughout nineteenth-century holiness circles. At a series of evangelistic meetings in Oregon in 1918, Harold Stephens had declared to one congregation:

> Every person in this church, and every other church, too, should realize that without the Holy Spirit the church must fail. The Spirit gives us faith and courage. He makes us strong. He sends us on our way rejoicing. Let the church people become more and more imbued with this Spirit and the church will be what Christ meant it should be.

Through the Stephens brothers, large numbers of men and women in North America experienced conversion and became passionate for evangelism and Christian service in society.

Revival and opposition
When Harold Stephens and his wife came to Calvary Baptist in Toronto in early 1919, they brought the same message of total commitment to Christ,

and that anything less was displeasing to the Holy Spirit. But this message seems to have disturbed some of the leadership of the church, though the pastor, Donald MacIntyre, was fully in line with it as were many in the congregation.

There is no explicit evidence that those leaders who opposed the message of Harold Stephens were motivated by liberal theological ideas, but it may well have been that laxity in theology had led to laxity in thinking about Christian discipleship. But the men and women who deeply appreciated the preaching of Harold Stephens were on fire for Jesus and found it difficult to restrain their disagreement with many of the leadership of the church. And as is often the case in times of spiritual awakening—large or small—a division resulted between those who embraced the revival and those who did not.

About sixty men and women left Calvary to form a new congregation, which would come to be called Forward Baptist Church, and which celebrated its hundredth anniversary in 2019. At the heart of the new local church were three things: a solid commitment to the Word of God, a hunger to worship Christ, and a passion to see the lost saved. In the century that followed, this church would see over a hundred of their congregation commissioned as cross-cultural missionaries, and at times the monies given to missions amounted to well over a third of the annual budget.

James A. Grant, pastor of St Clair Avenue Baptist Church in Toronto, preached at the church's first communion on Sunday evening, July 6, 1919. As he preached and the congregation of fifty or so then celebrated the Lord's Supper for the first time as a distinct body of believers, it was recorded in the church minutes that "the presence of the Holy Spirit was felt in power by the whole congregation."

Needing the presence of the Spirit of God
While we might have some disagreement with Harold Stephens about the work of the Holy Spirit, surely he was right to insist that without the presence of the Holy Spirit we can do nothing for Christ or his kingdom. Oh, to know that blessed presence in all our gatherings as did those Toronto Baptists a hundred or so years ago!

Index

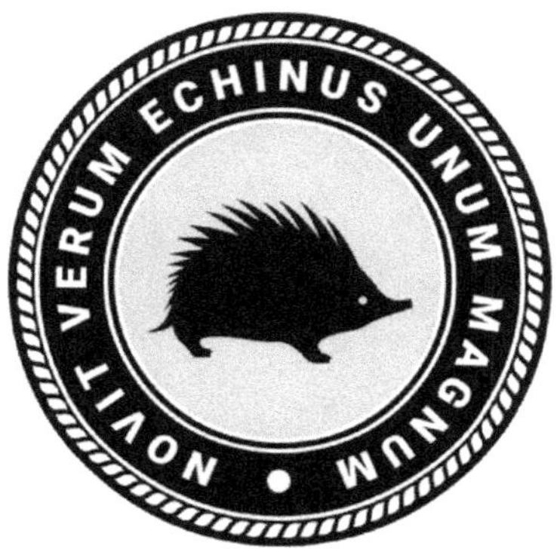

Among the fragmentary sayings of the ancient Greek author Archilochus, born on the Greek island of Paros in the eighth/seventh century BC, is this cryptic statement, πόλλ᾽ οἶδ᾽ ἀλώπηξ, ἀλλ᾽ ἐχῖνος ἕν μέγα ("the fox knows many things, but the hedgehog knows one great thing"). The Dutch theologian Erasmus later translated the Greek into Latin thus: *Multa novit vulpes, verum echinus unum magnum.* The saying was given a degree of currency in the modern day by its use in a famous essay by Isaiah Berlin entitled *The Hedgehog and the Fox* (Weidenfeld and Nicolson, 1953), in which he divided historians and thinkers into foxes, those authors whose thought has no central focus, and hedgehogs, those thinkers and historians who subsume their thought under one great idea. The Andrew Fuller Center for Baptist Studies, of which the author, Michael Haykin, is the director, took a portion of this saying—*novit verum echinus unum magnum*—for its motto a few years ago.

"Historian Michael A.G. Haykin welcomes us into his world of historical peculiarities, fascinating biographies, and intriguing stories. These enriching readings provide a window into divine providence as it unfolds in God's grand redemptive history. While scholarly in substance, *The Weekly Historian* is wonderfully readable, carefully accessible, and will no doubt ignite your curiosity for more as you discover your place in God's story."

Dustin Benge, Associate Professor of Biblical Spirituality and Historical Theology, The Southern Baptist Theological Seminary, Louisville, KY; Senior Fellow of The Andrew Fuller Center for Baptist Studies.

"*The Weekly Historian: 52 Reflections on Christian History* is the latest book from the prolific pen of Michael A.G. Haykin. The book is a 'taster of the riches of the past history of Christianity.' This 'taster' will whet your appetite for more such nourishing food from the banquet table of church history, one covered with scrolls, books, pen, and ink. From papyrus to purple and from Macarius to Spurgeon, you will encounter fascinating subjects and intriguing characters in *Weekly*. My favorite chapter is 'A Frantic Passion for Purple.' Haykin's interest in color is not the odd curiosity of an out-of-touch historian, but a lesson in the providence of God in the advancement of the gospel. I plan to read *The Weekly Historian* to my daughters and I anticipate loving every minute of such a happy endeavor. Read this book for the sheer pleasure of the experience but also as a means to better understand the present and to more courageously face the future via these delightful stories of the past."

Ray Rhodes, Jr., author of *Yours, till Heaven, the Untold Love Story of Charles and Susie Spurgeon* and *Susie: The Life and Legacy of Susannah Spurgeon* from Moody Publishers. He is also author of an upcoming biography of Charles Spurgeon, scheduled for 2024 from B&H Academic.

"Imagine going on a sight-seeing tour alongside a world-renowned photographer. What sort of pictures would he take? and would you not be eager to see the treasure trove of his camera roll? It is in much the same vein that one might view Dr. Michael A.G. Haykin's sight-seeing tour through church history in his latest gem, *The Weekly Historian*. This book is a delicious feast of history and theology through the eye and pen of one of our most eminent modern divines. Each entry is full of intrigue, insight, and inspiration. Any library without this book is incomplete."

Nate Pickowicz, pastor of Harvest Bible Church, Gilmanton Iron Works, New Hampshire; author of the upcoming *R.C. Sproul: Defender of the Reformed Faith* (H&E, 2022).

"In *The Weekly Historian: 52 Reflections on Church History*, Dr. Michael Haykin agrees with the eighteenth-century Baptist leader, Caleb Evans, that 'Every Christian ought to be a good historian.' This book will help. While not an exhaustive survey, *The Weekly Historian* is a trusted guide into some of the most important people and events of church history. Haykin's expertise allows him to do fine history in accessible snapshots that will spur the reader on to further study and a deeper appreciation for the Christian's shared history—a most noble enterprise."

Michael E. Pohlman, Associate Professor of Preaching and Pastoral Ministry and Chair, Department of Ministry and Proclamation, The Southern Baptist Theological Seminary; co-host of the weekly podcast *Bede: History for the Church*.